ractice

"*Work as a Spiritual Practice* is full of excellent, wise, simple advice to transform work into awakening. Lewis Richmond really shows how Right Livelihood is possible in almost any job. Bravo!"

—Jack Kornfield, author of *Buddha's Little Instruction Book*

"Richmond gives us tangible ways to recognize meaningful moments of our work lives and value those moments. Only by doing so can we begin to see the magic in events that are otherwise mundane."

—*Rocky Mountain News*

"Richmond . . . does an excellent job of explaining the principles of Buddhism and relating them to the workplace. The book is filled with illustrative stories that make the reading enlightening for those seeking more than just a paycheck."

—*Washington Times*

A Practical

Buddhist Approach

to Inner Growth

and Satisfaction

on the Job

Work as a Spiritual Practice

LEWIS
RICHMOND

BROADWAY BOOKS
New York

BROADWAY

A hardcover edition of this book was published in 1999 by
Broadway Books.

Broadway Books titles may be purchased for business or
promotional use or for special sales. For information, please write
to: Special Markets Department, Random House, Inc., 1540
Broadway, New York, NY 10036.

BROADWAY BOOKS and its logo, a letter B bisected on the diagonal,
are trademarks of Broadway Books, a division of Random House, Inc.

First trade paperback edition published 2000.

Designed by Lee Fukui

Grateful acknowledgment is made for permission to reprint the
following:
Page 6: Permission granted by Ann Landers and Creators
Syndicate.
Page 45: From *Letters to a Young Poet* by Rainer Maria Rilke,
translated by Stephen Mitchell. Copyright © 1984 by Stephen
Mitchell. Reprinted by permission of Random House, Inc.
Page 62: From *Healing Anger: The Power of Patience from a Buddhist
Perspective* by H. H. the Dalai Lama, 1997, Snow Lion Publications,
Ithaca, NY.
Page 93: From *The Farther Shore* by Don Gifford. Reprinted by
permission of the Atlantic Monthly Press.

Library of Congress Cataloging-in-Publication Data
Richmond, Lewis, 1947–
Work as a spiritual practice: a practical Buddhist approach to
inner growth and satisfaction on the job / by Lewis Richmond.
p.   cm.
1. Religious life—Buddhism. 2 Work—Religious aspects–
Buddhism. 3. Buddhism—Doctrines. I. Title.
BQ5400.R53   1998
294.3'444—dc21   98–30814
                    CIP

ISBN 0-7679-0233-5

00 01 02 03 04 10 9 8 7 6 5 4 3 2 1

To

my teacher and

lifelong inspiration

SHUNRYU SUZUKI ROSHI

PART ONE: INTRODUCTION
THE SHINY BLUE GRASSSHOPPER   1

The world is full of spiritual opportunity, symbolized by the shiny blue grasshopper sitting on the Buddha's head, or your coworker's head, or your own head. Where is the grasshopper now?

1 | The Koan of Everyday Life   5

A koan is a spiritual question or problem. We needn't look afar for such questions; everyday life is full of them. Even the ringing phone presents

Contents

us with spiritual opportunity. The next time the phone rings, the person on the other end of the line could be you.

2 | What Is a Spiritual Practice?   13

Spiritual practice is not a rehearsal but an end in itself, an activity that changes us inside and reverberates in the soul. It is a way to refine and develop our character, which is the deep, stable part of ourselves that others can rely on. Character counts.

3 | The Energy Wheel   21

The Energy Wheel is a map of our mental and emotional experiences. Divided into four sectors—Conflict, Inspiration, Accomplishment, and Stagnation—it teaches us that moment after moment, day after day, for the whole of our life, we move around and through the Wheel.

PART TWO: CONFLICT   29

4 | Stress   33

Even in the most frenetic job, we can learn to cultivate and maintain an awareness of the body and breathing, establish small rituals of care in our movements—while walking down the hall, picking up the phone, or talking in a meeting—and create a "self-mantra" to focus our awareness.

Making Your Own Luck, we can move through discouragement and sustain our deeper life.

ling by Paying Attention—that paradoxically encourages us to give up ordinary control and, by trusting in Simultaneity and Interdependence, allow the situation itself to guide us.

Generosity is a tangible expression of the self's openness, of our willingness to feel other people's sorrow and desire other people's happiness. The practices of Right Speech, Gentle Truth, Presence, and Seeing and Hearing with the Heart are all efforts we can make on the job to offer generosity to our colleagues.

Buddhism teaches that the whole universe is like a net of jewels, in which each jewel reflects all the others, and that each of us is one of the jewels in the net. This realization leads us to feel and express a deep gratitude for everyone and everything in our domain, from our coworkers to the bits of broken glass in the parking lot. The Buddhist teaching of Right Livelihood in today's interconnected, global economy is most comprehensible as *conscious* livelihood.

It is a rare person who can really handle power. Power corrupts because each of us wants to be the star of a fairy tale in which every wish comes true. Outer Power, based on money, rank, knowledge, and status, seems to rule the world, but Inner Power, rooted in spiritual values, ethics, and character, is stronger.

On the edge of a new century, what can we all do to transform the dominant system of human commerce—free-market capitalism—so that it includes and embraces spiritual as well as material values?

Here is a visualization practice to see the place where we work as a sanctuary or temple and every one of our coworkers as having a shining jewel in their foreheads.

This book contains many voices besides my own—not only the participants in my workshops whose stories appear on nearly every page, but the many working people I have met in my travels, each of whom had something important to teach me. My heartfelt thanks to every one of them.

Acknowledgments

My agent Eileen Cope saw the possibility of this book lurking within me well before I was able to see it in myself. Many thanks for her midwifery and unbridled enthusiasm! Stephanie Gunning provided invaluable editorial help in the early stages, continuing to ask "But what is this book *about?*" until I could provide a satisfactory answer not only to her but to myself.

Thanks too to those friends and family who undertook the yeoperson's task of reading the manuscript—Sylvia Boorstein, Lama Surya Das, Steve Tipton, and my wife, Amy. Their unconditional support and helpful criticisms were invaluable in refining the voice and tone of each chapter and story.

I am most grateful to all the people at Broadway Books whose vision and hard work helped create the finished product, especially my editor Suzanne Oaks, who understood this book from the inside. Her knack for knowing what parts needed to go where was a great help in shaping and clarifying the book as a whole.

Finally, I want to acknowledge a debt I can never repay to my Buddhist teacher Shunryu Suzuki Roshi. I have met a great many Buddhist teachers over the years, but few if any whose depth of character and insight was so clear and palpable as Suzuki Roshi's. Though he died in 1972, I continue to learn from him every day.

part one

INTRODUCTION

The Shiny Blue
Grasshopper

May all beings be awake.
May all beings be happy.
May all beings be at peace.

UNIVERSAL PRAYER FOR THE
WELFARE OF ALL BEINGS

ONE MORNING in late September, during our Wednesday meditation group, a grasshopper began to make its slow way in the predawn shadows across the hardwood floor. As I watched out of the corner of my eye I wondered, "How does the grasshopper know where to go?" From his vantage point, the floor was huge and featureless, like an ocean. One direction was much like another. He could even come to me. I wondered if he would.

Slowly, at insect speed, crawling, not hopping, he made his way past all of us and vanished into the shadows.

Later, when I was giving a talk, I mentioned the grasshopper, and asked, "How does he know where to go?" This is a big question. How do any of us know where to go? How do we know what to do? What choices to make? Where to work? Whom to love? How to live?

As I was finishing the talk, I turned to gesture toward the small wooden Buddha statue on the altar, and there, to everyone's amazement, perched on the top of the Buddha's head, was the grasshopper, shiny blue-green in the sunlight now streaming through the windows.

This is a true story. I am not making it up, or even exaggerating a bit. Six other people were there, and they can tell you. But why should you even wonder? This sort of small miracle happens all the time. It happens to me, and it happens to you. It is all around us. Why did the grasshopper seek out the top of the Buddha? Was he attracted by the light of the candle? Was he trying to find safety from the cat we heard meowing in the doorway earlier?

These are explanations, but they miss the point. The point is not to say "Wow! What a miracle! How special, how spiritual!" but simply to note that this is the way the world is. Shiny blue grasshoppers are always lighting on top of the heads of Buddhas, or on top of my head or your head or your boss's head or your coworker's head. It is not a matter of miracles, but a matter of noticing.

When I read reports of people who claim to see the image of the Virgin Mary on the side of a building, or in the patterns in the stump of an old oak tree, the stories usually include an explanation from a scientific expert about glass refraction or oak fungi. Who does that expert think the Virgin Mary is? A person who lived two thousand years ago and who therefore cannot *really* be there? A person who lives *only* in someone's imagination? What does the word *really* mean? What does *being there* mean? What is imagination, and how is it less real than glass refraction?

These issues are far more interesting as questions than as answers, because as questions they open up our life, they make it shimmer, they make it sunlit and translucent. They allow us to notice the shiny blue grasshopper even at work, even on the highway, even when we are tired and discouraged.

The shiny blue grasshopper is what we live for, and work for, and love for. And although shiny blue grasshoppers can be found everywhere, this book is about finding them in the workplace, at our jobs, among our coworkers, scattered throughout our places of employment. It is about how to make our work life shine.

As we were taking down the altar and putting away the cushions and mats, I carried the Buddha statue to the window, with the grasshopper still on it, and let the grasshopper hop down onto the windowsill. It remained there for a moment, still as a stone, and then slowly, deliberately, it spread its wings and was gone.

But not entirely gone. From that moment on, the grasshopper was within me and all who were there and saw it come and go. And now that I have told you about it, the grasshopper is within you too. That is how the grasshopper moves among all of us.

If we could work together at our jobs with the feeling the grasshopper inspires in us, then the workplace might become a wonderful, joyful place. Even if we can't, the grasshopper is perched here and there, waiting for us to notice.

Where is the grasshopper now?

"So. What do you do?"

How many times have you been asked that question and answered, without thinking, "I'm a lawyer," or "I'm an aerobics instructor," or "I'm a musician." But beyond small talk, that question suggests a deeper inquiry. What, indeed, do you *DO*, here on this earth, here in your life? What is your work? What is your passion? What is your aspiration, your dream, your calling? Do you find joy in your work? Have you given up hoping that joy

is something you might expect from work? Or do you love your work so much that you have no time to enjoy anything else? Why do you have the job you do? Is it just a way to make ends meet, or is it something more? What is the relationship between your inner self and your outer, public life on the job?

This book seeks to guide you on a path of spiritual discovery about the work that you do and offer practical ways to make that work more connected to your inner life. I don't know if what you learn will improve your job in a conventional sense. Who knows, it might make you upset enough to quit your job and find a better one! But it may help you in a spiritual sense.

I am a Buddhist, which means I am also a realist. In our society, work is not expected to

To find joy in your work is the greatest thing for a human being.

HARRY ROBERTS: agronomist, cowboy, woodworker, welder, boxer, gun-sight maker, spiritual teacher in the Native American tradition, and Ginger Rogers's dance partner be spiritually satisfying. For the most part, our jobs are designed to make someone somewhere a profit. Listen to what one recent writer to Ann Landers had to say about his job:

> Why should anybody give their best effort on the job? No one cares about the worker anymore. Growing up in the '60s, we were taught that giving your best would always ensure your employment. That's baloney. It's all a matter of random chance whether or not your job continues. I've been laid off twice through no fault of my own.

Perhaps someday work will evolve to the point where it is once again integrated with family, community, spirituality, and nature, as it was in preindustrial times. Until then, the Buddhist worldview begins with today, just as it is, for good and ill—today's job, today's life, today's "you."

What this book offers are ways to help you become more aware, more awake, and more engaged in your work life. Even the worst job has its compensations, and even the greatest job has its demerits. This book can't make your job perfect, but it may make it more workable. The reason I think so is because, spiritually speaking, you are in charge. Your employer may dictate every aspect of your work life, but no matter what kind of job you do, you are the boss of your inner life.

Most people think of Buddhists as people who meditate. That's partly true. I spent many years living in a Buddhist retreat center, where I did indeed spend many hours each day in silent meditation. But Buddhism has its active side too, and some of its practices are adaptable to a busy, engaged life. Many of them aren't meditation in the usual sense of the word but rather exercises in awareness and focus. Some address various emotional states, such as anger, fear, frustration, and boredom. Others work on how we interact with people, or on the speed and pace of our activity. All of them are designed to awaken the fundamental spiritual inquiry: Who am I? What am I doing here? How can I fulfill my life's potential? These practices are all based on the conviction that we have the resources we need to make that inquiry come to life, and that the circumstances of our daily life can be the raw materials in that effort.

One thing's for sure: You don't have to *be* a Buddhist to benefit from these practices. During my career as a meditation teacher, I have taught and practiced with Catholic monks, rabbis, Protestant ministers, Muslims, nature worshipers, agnostics, atheists—people of many religious and nonreligious persuasions, many of whom, I'm sure, didn't think of themselves as Buddhists. But they all benefited from Buddhist practices.

WORK LIFE AND SPIRITUAL LIFE

Have you ever heard the saying "It's not my wife and it's not my life"? It's something to say when things go badly at work. Well, your job may not be your wife (or husband), but it *is* your life, or a big part of it. Studies show that the average American is working 150 more hours a year than in 1910—a sobering thought! When we disassociate ourselves from our work by saying, in effect, "This is not the part of my life that really counts, I just do this for a living," we close ourselves off from what my teacher Harry Roberts used to say was the greatest thing for a human being—to find joy in our work.

How do you feel about your job? Do you love your work but find that it takes up so much of your time that it really *is* your whole life? Or, is your work dull and drab, but you don't mind because you are going to night school to prepare for a different, more satisfying career? Perhaps you work in the helping professions or in education, and it is not your boss but your clients (or patients, or students, or parents) who drive you to distraction.

Regardless of your situation, there are certain characteristics of work that are universal. Unless you work at home, you travel to work. When you get there, you perform some task, such as computer programming, carpentry, or management, for which you are financially rewarded. You interact with other people in an environment where power is unequally shared. Your job performance is measured in some way. You compete with others for rewards. You can quit your job. You can lose your job. And you have (we hope) a life outside your job.

Let's contrast this description of life on the job with the life of the spirit. In our spiritual life, we are not in competition with anyone else for spiritual rewards. How well or badly we do is beside the point. We honor and appreciate all people (including ourselves!) for their intrinsic humanity. We care for others, we share and are generous, we forgive. The world of the spirit is not a matter of bonuses, promotions, or awards. Advancement is not the point. We are already whole and complete just as we are.

So it would seem that spiritual life is close to the opposite of work life! But suppose we stop for a moment and ask ourselves why the modern workplace is the way it is. Is it because evil tyrants created the modern workplace to torment us? Or is it because over the last few hundred years people have cooperated to create a world in which we live better, longer, and happier, and can provide a more secure future for our children? We are all collectively responsible for the way work is today, and to whatever extent that situation is far from perfect, we must keep exploring, experimenting, and trying. It may be that over time the nature of work will undergo some grand transformation. Some social theorists think that kind of change is already under way. I think so too, and in chapter 19, "The Transformation of Work," I explore some of those trends. But let's not wait for that great moment. Today there is something we can do. Today we can make a change. Today it is possible to make a difference.

As you begin exploring this book—and you need not read it from front to back; it is designed to be browsed—I ask you to make only one commitment, and that is to trust yourself. Trust your own instincts, your intuition, your judgment. The knowledge you need to change your work life for the better is already within you. Set aside, for now, the notion that on the job you work for somebody else. In your spiritual life, you are self-employed. You work for yourself. No one need know about this inner job. It can be your secret. Whatever efforts you make will be outside the realm of success or failure. I don't know what will happen if you try the practices in this book, but I am sure of one thing: *Something* will happen.

The reason I am so sure is that something is always happening. The world is full of spiritual opportunity. The trick is to be alert enough to notice it. That is the real work, and the joy of work, and if we catch on to that trick, it doesn't matter in the short run what our day job is. In the end, if we are kind to ourselves, our efforts will be fruitful.

THE KOAN OF EVERYDAY LIFE

But what kind of fruit will it be? A raise, a better job, a happier work and home life? Perhaps, but not necessarily. Spiritual practice is more about questions than answers, more about searching than finding, more about effort than accomplishment. In one school of Buddhism, those who practice ponder spiritual questions called *kōans*. There are hundreds of memorable stories, usually taken from the lives of ancient Buddhist teachers, that are used as koans. Some of them have even become part of popular culture. For instance, the question "What is the sound of one hand clapping?" was featured in an episode of *The Simpsons* television show.

In addition to these prefabricated questions, there is another kind of koan, called the koan of everyday life. Human life itself, the mystery of being thrust into the world by birth and swept out of it by death, is an imponderable puzzle, one that we can try to ignore but cannot escape. So much of what passes for "ordinary" life is, when seen through different eyes, not ordinary at all, but full of potential for spiritual learning. To practice the koan of everyday life means to confront every situation as though it were a profound spiritual question. In that sense, every koan story is a specific instance of the koan of everyday life.

One such koan story goes like this:

A monk asked his teacher, "What is the Buddha?" and the teacher answered, "The cypress tree in the garden."

What does it mean? What does a cypress tree have to do with Buddha, that is, our awakened self? Let's imagine this cypress tree, spreading over the path in the monastery garden. What could be more ordinary, or familiar, than the aged tree that each monk passed every day for the whole of his life? In that sense, the cypress tree means the most familiar thing. What familiar thing do you pass? Is it your kitchen table? Your car? Your good friend? Your spouse or children? Your coworkers? The copy machine in the office corner?

This book is based on the premise that our ordinary routine contains numerous treasures and the details of our workday, from the morning commute to the coffee break, the lunch hour, the afternoon meetings, the evening ride home, contain within them any number of gifts for our spirit, if only we would allow ourselves to receive them.

Here is a true story to illustrate this.

A woman named Julie managed a customer service department in an insurance company. Because of budget cuts, in addition to her managerial responsibilities, she had to spend a couple of hours each day taking overflow calls. The worst part of her job, she told me, was the unpredictable ringing of the telephone. As the week went on, she found herself resenting that sound more and more. She would try to turn the volume down, but if it got too soft she couldn't hear it in time, which was even worse.

One day, without really thinking about it, she found herself pushing the button to lower the volume on the phone in rhythm with the ringing itself and suddenly thought, "I'm the one doing the ringing." From then on, every time the ringing got on her nerves, she would raise and lower the volume of the ringing in time with the ringing, as though her finger were making the phone ring.

"It's a silly thing," she said, "but it made me feel in charge again."

In this case the koan of everyday life took the form of a ringing phone. Anyone who works in an office understands only too well how large that ringing phone can loom. We all have to deal with it, none of us likes it, and yet that ringing phone can be a wake-up call to our inner life. In having to confront the irritation of the ringing phone, we also confront the fundamentals of who we are and want to be. The ringing phone stands for everything in our life that we cannot control, everything that makes our life unpredictable, confusing, and difficult. For those of us who think of spiritual life as something to be found in a church, a retreat center, or a walk by the seashore, the ringing phone is the last thing we wish to hear.

But for those who are willing to see a spiritual opportunity in the ordinariness of everyday circumstance, the ringing phone is no less profound an encounter than the cypress tree in the garden.

What makes the difference is the resource of spiritual practice, which is a way to transform the mundane into the sacred, the ordinary into the profound. In Julie's case, her instinct to embrace the ringing not as something outside but as something inside was an example of a practice we will be exploring later as "Seeing and Hearing with the Heart." She was hearing that phone not with her mundane ear, but with a more spiritual organ.

To understand that a sound is not something outside ourselves, but something within, is a shift of consciousness that can lead to a different understanding of who we are for others and who others are for us. From that insight comes generosity, compassion, and wisdom.

It may not seem like such a great accomplishment to tap our fingers in time with the ringing of a phone. But spiritual learning is nothing other than the accumulation, over time, of such small, modest awakenings. Eventually this can lead to a fundamental shift of perspective, a change in the sense of who "I" am and what "the world" is.

It is said that the monk, on hearing the words *the cypress tree in the garden,* experienced such a shift in perspective. In understanding such a story, it is important to realize how intimately that tree was a part of the monk's daily life, just as the ringing phone was a part of Julie's. The cypress tree in the garden was already in his heart. He passed it every day as he carried water to the kitchen, or firewood to the bathhouse, just as we might pass the office copier or the paper cup dispenser as we walk down the hall. That is why hearing the words *the cypress tree in the garden* caused his heart to open. Through spiritual practice, through concentrated attention over a long period of time, the tree was already growing within him.

The cypress tree in the garden can be anything, as long as we really see it and hear it, are open to it, and have an alert, caring, questioning mind.

This is the koan of everyday life. This is the potential of the workplace to be, for each of us, a spiritual place. This is the world seen with the eyes of awakening, a world in which everything we see and touch is offered to us as a gift.

Lift your eyes from this page, look up, look around you. Notice the first thing you see. What is it? A desk lamp? A window shade? A pencil? These humble objects are, indeed, capable of becoming your close spiritual friends.

Greet them as friends, because as you peruse this book, they will befriend as well as challenge you.

If nothing else, the next time the phone rings I hope that you will remember Julie, her tapping finger, the monk, and the cypress tree, and consider the possibility that the voice on the other end of the line might be someone other than the person who placed the call.

It might be you yourself.

When I was a boy, I was a serious piano student and practiced after school at least two hours a day, sometimes more. I can still hear my mother calling out from the kitchen, "Stop fiddling around! Practice!" She was a music teacher by profession, so there was no fooling her! That's what we usually mean by "practice"—practice the piano, practice our golf swing, practice a public speech. That kind of practice is a rehearsal, or a way to perfect a skill.

Spiritual practice is not like this. A spiritual practice is not a warm-up or rehearsal but an end in itself, an activity that expresses and develops our inner life. Spiritual practices are easier to describe than define, so let me offer you some familiar examples.

Catholics cross themselves. Observant Jews keep kosher. People of various religions say grace at meals or fast for periods of time. These are familiar examples of spiritual practices. Wearing a wedding ring is a less obvious example, but it is a visible expression of the marriage vow. Saying "Bless you!" when someone sneezes was originally a prayer for protection against evil. Saying "Good-bye" (a shortened form of "God be with you") was once a blessing too.

Spiritual practice is not a rehearsal but an end in itself, an activity that changes us inside and reverberates in the soul.

And, of course, throughout the world, the most common spiritual practice of all is prayer.

For some people, such practices are embedded in their daily lives, as part of their religious identities. Others may feel alienated from such practices, perhaps because they seem hollow and mechanical, or are associated with feelings of guilt and duty. This is unfortunate, because the true intent of a spiritual practice is not about mechanically obeying rules but developing an awareness of the sacred. Keeping kosher, for example, is partly about respecting and honoring the food we eat and how it comes to us. Making the sign of the cross is a way to physically express a connection with the suffering of Jesus. Blessing someone when he or she sneezes shows sympathy and concern. These are not just empty rituals. They have the potential to change us inside, to develop our character and make us more aware of our larger responsibility to ourselves, to others, and to God.

Many such practices are unique to their own tradition. For example, Catholics do not keep kosher, nor do Jews cross themselves. But there are many spiritual practices that can be done by people of any religion, or no religion. Buddhism is particularly rich in such practices, which is one reason why it has attracted so much interest in the West. Buddhism traditionally emphasized practice over doctrine and belief. In fact, we might say that its practices *are* its beliefs. In that sense, it can be thought of not only as a religion in its own right but also as a "toolset" for a religion. Just as a hammer, a saw, or a pair of pliers each has a specific purpose, each of Buddhism's many spiritual practices is designed to work on some aspect of our character and inner life.

THE REASON FOR SPIRITUAL PRACTICE

Our spiritual self asks root questions: Who am I? Why am I here? What is my purpose? A spiritual practice is something that we DO (as opposed to something that we believe) that helps us confront these questions. It is an activity that changes us inside, that reverberates in the soul.

In our love life, we look for passion, companionship, and intimacy. In our family life, we make a home, raise children, and take care of our relatives. In our work life, we build a career, make money, and contribute our energies to some enterprise. Our spiritual life is our deepest and most comprehensive life, enfolding all these other lives like a cloak or vestment. Regardless of how outwardly successful we are, our spiritual life determines the kind of person we really are—a person of generosity, authority, and satisfaction, or a person haunted by insecurity and fear.

At one time I studied with Harry Roberts, who was part Irish and part Native American. He gained spiritual knowledge from his uncle, a traditional medicine man. When Harry was a small boy, he watched while his uncle sewed feathers into a headdress used for a traditional dance ceremony. He was puzzled as he watched his uncle pull apart a whole section he had already sewn and prepare to do it over again.

"Why are you taking it apart?" Harry asked. "The dance is at night. Nobody will see it. Who will know?"

"I will know," his uncle replied.

For Harry's uncle, sewing that headdress was not just a job. What mattered was not just the appearance of the headdress but also his state of mind while he sewed it. As a spiritual leader of his community, it was not enough for him to do a passable job. It had to be good enough to satisfy his own sense of inner worth as well. That, much more than the headdress itself, was what he would bring to the ceremonial dance. Sewing the headdress was not about stitches or embroidery. It was about spirit, about responsibility, and about character. It was a spiritual practice.

CHARACTER COUNTS

When was the last time you said that someone was a person of good character? Perhaps you said it in a courtroom or in an employment reference letter. To talk about someone's "character" in that way is a bit old-fashioned. We are more likely to use the word in the phrase

"What a character!" or when we speak of the "character" that an actor played in a film.

Character in its formal sense means the solid, rooted, interior part of ourselves, not our exterior personality, but the part of us that carries our values, our ethics, and our convictions. Other people can count on our character, because it is not made up, not put on, not an act.

Character is not a fashion statement or a hairstyle. It is not something built in a day but rather the sum total of how we have lived our life, the choices we have made, the lessons we have learned from our parents and teachers, as well as the challenges we have faced.

Character is what comes to the fore in times of crisis. Under duress, our surface personality falls away. There is no time to think "What is the right thing to do or say?" The voice that speaks in such moments is the Voice of Truth, the unalloyed reality of who we are. It is also the part of ourselves we can most deeply share with others. That is why it was so important to Harry's uncle that he come to the ceremonial dance in the right state of mind. He was a leader of his community. His character was something that other people depended on and drew strength from. He couldn't fool anybody. Who he was would be evident for all to see. If he cut corners in the sewing of the headdress, if he imagined that what he did with the needle and thread was something inconsequential and private, he would be cheating his people and letting everyone down.

It may seem that the modern workplace doesn't recognize character in that way. As long as we perform well, do our job, and fulfill our employer's expectations, who we are deep inside is just a private matter.

That is how it seems on the surface. In reality, character always makes a difference. Character is what allows us to take charge of our inner life. It gives us strength, helps us face adversity and injustice, and keeps us calm when chaos reigns.

My own experience of business relationships is that they depend on character a good deal more than most of us would like to admit. I often have to negotiate complex contracts, but in the midst of all the nitpicking I am aware that in the end a contract only defines the terms under which the parties can sue each other. If it comes to that, the relationship has already failed. To be successful, a business relationship must be built on some amount of trust, and trust depends on character.

Though the workplace may rely on character, its importance is not often explicitly acknowledged. All the more reason for us to make our own efforts to cultivate character. When we treat character as important, then character comes alive for everyone around us. To the extent the workplace lacks heart, our effort to develop character can help restore its heart. To the extent the workplace makes demands on us that we cannot reasonably fulfill, character can help us do the best we can. Character is one answer to the questions: Who am I? What am I doing here?

Character counts.

EVERYTHING IS ALIVE

In the 1970 movie *Little Big Man,* a young pioneer boy was captured and raised by Native Americans. His stepfather was chief of the tribe. One day, the chief tried to explain to the boy the difference between white people, whom the chief called "crazy ones," and the Native Americans, whom the chief referred to in his language as "human beings."

"The difference between the crazy ones and human beings," the chief said, "is that the crazy ones think everything is dead, and we human beings think everything is alive."

Everything is alive! Not just plants and animals but stones, rivers, the sky, clouds, the dancing dust motes in a ray of sunlight. That sense of aliveness is the ground of spiritual life. Many people come to traditions like Buddhism in the hope of having such an experience and believe that the reason for spiritual practice is to make it happen. But spiritual practice is not just a means to make everything come alive.

Everything is already alive.

In that sense, spiritual practice is not a means to an end but an end in itself, a way to express ourselves fully and completely. The poet Wallace Stevens once said, "The true religious force in the world is not the church but the world itself." Churches, temples, and retreat centers are important. To belong to some spiritual community allows us to share our spiritual life with others and be encouraged by others. But we should also remember that everything in the world, even the fax machine that hums in the corner of the office, even the trash can next to it, bulging with Pepsi cans and crumpled paper, is already sacred. An old Pepsi can is one of those things that we dismiss as unimportant, as throwaway, as waste. But through spiritual practice we can come to understand what the chief in *Little Big Man* was trying to say. Everything is important. Everything has its place. Everything is sacred.

My first Buddhist teacher, Shunryu Suzuki Roshi, was once asked, "Why do we do meditation?"

He answered, "To polish our character."

To polish something is to make it shine. Polishing our character is not that different from polishing anything—a wood carving, a silver candlestick, a glass lens, an inlaid tabletop, a model clipper ship. Why do we want anything to shine? Why do we want ourselves to shine? For the joy of it, I think. I can't think of a better reason.

Why do such things give us joy as human beings? Why are we made the way we are? I cannot answer such questions. Spiritual practice is not about why, it is all about how.

SPIRITUAL PRACTICE IN THE WORKPLACE

Even people who are comfortable with the notion of spiritual practice are skeptical when I say that it can be done not just at home or at a retreat center but in the workplace. This book is based on the premise that it can be done, that the circumstances and challenges of our work life can be transformed into opportunities for inner growth. I want you to come away from reading this book with a sense that your inner life need not be compartmentalized into your own time, but that it can be alive and active all the time, even in the workplace. I want you to feel that, whether you love your job or hate it, you can be awake and aware in your work. I want to redefine the term *job satisfaction* to mean not a job where everything goes well and we rise quickly to the top but a job where we can grow, develop, and mature as human beings, regardless of what happens.

I spent the first fifteen years of my adult life as a Buddhist priest and meditation teacher and the second fifteen as a business executive, entrepreneur, and musician/composer. I was fortunate to have all that time for formal spiritual training. But even so, the deepest spiritual lessons I learned were out in the world—during the second fifteen years, not the first.

After I left the monastery and meditation hall, I kept asking myself, "How well does my spiritual training work in the workplace, in the schoolroom, in the family, in government, in personal relationships? How can it be applied?" My purpose in writing this book is to share some of the practices and techniques I have used, both in my own life and in the classes and workshops I have taught, to help me answer these questions.

From one point of view, the modern workplace is far from the ideal environment for spiritual development. It values competition, efficiency, technology, and profit. In contrast, the spiritual realm is about meaning, wholeness, connection, and cooperation. At first blush, we might think that the two worlds could not be further apart. But jobs are not performed by robots but by people like you and me, each of whom, beneath a veneer of rank, title, and status, shares the same fundamental desire for purpose, meaning, and a life that contributes something of value to the world.

Granted, the modern workplace doesn't make it easy to maintain a spiritual perspective while the phone rings, the fax machine whines, and we are asked to do ten hours' work in eight hours' time. All the more reason for us to rise up and embrace the workplace not as a roadblock but as an opportunity to say not "Thank God it's Friday" but "Thank God it's today." The practices I talk about in this book are more than techniques. They are ways to see work with different eyes, to focus on the part of our work that is beyond failure and success. When we feel that our inner life disappears at work, it is not only because the demands of our job overwhelm it but also because we lose track of it and don't know how to find it, rekindle it, and nurture it.

No matter what frustrations and indignities erode our sense of outer worth on the job, inside we remain vividly alive. No matter how insecure our tenure at work, no one can hand a pink slip to our soul. No one can say to our inner life, "You're fired!" I will say it again: You are the boss of your inner life. You really are.

In this way, work is not just a paycheck, not just a job. Work can be, and is, a spiritual practice.

How many days old are you? If you are thirty-five years old, you have lived for 12,775 days. How many of them can you actually remember? We certainly remember the high points of our life—our first day of school, our first kiss, our triumphs and rewards—as well as the low points, perhaps our parents' divorce, a death in the family, a defeat, or a broken heart. But most of the days of our lives recede in our memory as relatively uneventful.

But suppose we had a way of keeping better track of our days? Suppose we could mark down on some gigantic calendar a single word that would characterize each day's dominant mood? And to keep it simple, suppose we limited ourselves to just four words: *stressful, inspiring, contented,* and *sad.* Can we picture our life of thirty-five years as a string of 12,775 pieces of popcorn, each marked with one of those four words? It might look something like this:

The fundamental spiritual question the Wheel presents to us is: Does the Wheel turn us, or do we turn the Wheel?

Day 10,143   Stressful
Day 10,144   Stressful
Day 10,145   Inspiring
Day 10,146   Sad
Day 10,147   Contented

The Energy Wheel

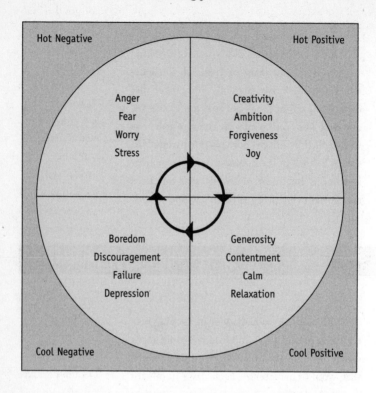

Hot Negative

Hot Positive

Anger
Fear
Worry
Stress

Creativity
Ambition
Forgiveness
Joy

Boredom
Discouragement
Failure
Depression

Generosity
Contentment
Calm
Relaxation

Cool Negative

Cool Positive

Or maybe every single day, all 12,775 of them, is marked "Contented"! If that's your life, then congratulations. You probably don't need this book!

Suppose we went further and gave each of the words a color: red for stressful, green for inspiring, golden for contented, and blue for sad. Then we could picture our imaginary calendar like those strings of colored popcorn children make for Christmas or Halloween. And what about the hours and minutes of each day—an hour of red, five minutes of blue, a half day of golden or green?

This is our life, constantly changing, constantly moving, never the same from one moment to the next. But how many of us really stop to ponder the significance of this colored string? Do we consider the way it changes from one day or hour to the next, the way we forget the color we just were—sad and blue a few hours ago and suddenly shining and golden on hearing some piece of good news? No matter how much we try to control our life, to protect ourselves and our loved ones from danger, to avoid sudden catastrophe, to remain safe and secure, there is no telling what the next moment will bring.

Even though our modern world has a host of miracles to help make our lives easier and more enjoyable—antibiotics, computers, cars, central heating, and stereo headphones—the fundamental facts of human life are the same today as they were one hundred, one thousand, or even five thousand years ago. What is so today will not be so tomorrow. Friends become enemies. Loved ones betray us. A child becomes sick, or dies. A secure job suddenly disappears. We lose everything we have gained, or make back everything we have lost.

This principle of continuous change is a central feature of Buddhist teaching, and its spiritual practices are in large part designed to help us grapple with it. Continuous change is a practical life problem, but it is also a core spiritual issue. How can we learn to embrace constant change in the details of our daily activity?

Over the centuries, generations of Buddhist monks have organized our various states of mind into a kind of map. On the preceding page is one modern version of that map, called the Energy Wheel. You can see that our four words—*stressful, inspiring, contented,* and *sad*—have become sectors of the Wheel. Their names—Conflict, Inspiration, Accomplishment, and Stagnation—have been made more generic, and the Wheel itself is divided along two axes—Hot/Cool and Positive/Negative—as follows:

HOT NEGATIVE (CONFLICT)	HOT POSITIVE (INSPIRATION)
Anger	Creativity
Fear	Ambition
Worry	Forgiveness
Stress	Joy

COOL NEGATIVE (STAGNATION)	COOL POSITIVE (ACCOMPLISHMENT)
Boredom	Generosity
Discouragement	Contentment
Failure	Calm
Depression	Relaxation

In this context, positive doesn't just mean "good," and negative doesn't mean "bad." These are not judgments but rather descriptions of how we feel. Positive states encourage us, while negative states hinder us. Positive states are ones that we like and want to continue, and negative states are ones we dislike and try to avoid. But all of these states can be opportunities for inner growth and change.

I live in northern California, where driving is a spacious, polite sort of exercise. But in New York City, as I am reminded whenever I take a taxi, driving can sometimes be a life-and-death sport. During one memorable thirty-minute ride from the Upper West Side to Greenwich Village, Ahmed, my cabbie, gave a vivid demonstration of all four sectors of the Energy Wheel. First, he screeched to a stop to avoid hitting a jaywalker in Times Square. When the jaywalker responded by thumping the hood of the cab and cursing loudly, Ahmed cursed back more loudly. (Conflict!) Then as we sat in stopped traffic for ten minutes, he passed the time by telling me how boring it was to drive a cab. "I just sit, all day long. Sit, sit, sit. That's what I do." (Stagnation!) Our next challenge was a cordoned-off area around the hotel where President Clinton was giving a speech. Faced with this ultimate challenge, Ahmed came to life, careening and weaving his way through side streets and even a drive-through parking garage to get around this obstacle, all the while keeping up an excited running patter. (Inspiration.) Finally we arrived at my destination. I felt a little unsteady as I stood up (Conflict again), but Ahmed had suddenly become relaxed, cheerful, and composed, probably because he saw in my hand a fat thankful-to-be-alive tip. (Accomplishment.) There it was—the whole panorama of human experience in one thirty-minute cab ride!

All of us experience this same kind of change and volatility in our own jobs. We might attend a morning staff meeting that leaves us irritable and anxious. Then, on picking up our phone messages, we unexpectedly hear some wonderful news, and our mood is transformed. Then we meet an old friend for lunch and are bored with her interminable chatter about boyfriends. Back at the office, our indispensable assistant has suddenly gone home sick. Cancel our evening plans! We're going to have to work late. Our earlier euphoria vanishes. We are irritable again.

The Energy Wheel is a way of organizing these various states of mind. The axis of positive and negative divides the mind into states that are unpleasant versus those that are pleasant. The axis of hot and cool describes the intensity of the energy. So, for example, anger is *qualitatively* a negative state—unpleasant, difficult, and painful. And *quantitatively* anger is intense, highly focused, and energized. At the opposite end of the spectrum, a state of relaxation is pleasurable as well as being spread out and diffuse. The Wheel represents the full range of our mental and emotional experiences.

It is a natural human tendency to want to spend as much time as possible in the Cool Positive portion of the Wheel, to be successful, accomplished, worry-free, relaxed, and peaceful. But that is not the way life is. The diagram is a Wheel rather than a straight line, because we circulate around it and through it, moving from one state to another, sometimes happy, sometimes sad, sometimes hot, sometimes cool.

Traditional Buddhist meditation places special emphasis on developing the Cool Positive portion of the Wheel, where we are calm, relaxed, and at peace. That certainly is one goal of meditation, but not the only one. The deeper purpose of meditation, and for that matter of all spiritual practice, is to be awake and aware in each state of mind and every life situation—in other words, to be comfortable with the whole Wheel.

I spent many years living in a spiritual community, an ideal environment for meditation and calm reflection. I feel fortunate to have had that opportunity and wish more people could have such an experience at some time in their lives. At the same time, I'm not sure a monastery is the best situation for mastering the whole Wheel, or if there is any prefabricated environment suitable for that task other than life itself. Among some Buddhist schools of ancient China, monks were expected to leave the monastery after their formal training was concluded. Only after years of travel and maturing life experience were they considered qualified to teach. Monks who had grown too attached to the monastic life were sometimes described as "demons of the dark cave."

One of the first things I noticed when I left the retreat center for the workaday world was the sheer energy level. Compared to the stately pace of the monastic day, punctuated by the peaceful sounds of bells and wood blocks, the world of work was a maelstrom. When Willie Sutton, the notorious bank robber, was asked why he robbed banks, he said, "Because that's where the money is," a reply that has passed into common parlance as a pearl of existential wisdom. When people ask me why I am writing a book about spiritual practice in the workplace, I take my cue from Willie Sutton and answer, "Because that is where the energy is."

The Wheel is a map of change and a guideline for continuous transformation. Every sector of the Wheel can flow into any other sector. So, for example, Hot Negative states—anger, worry, fear, stress—can transform themselves into Hot Positive ones, such as inspiration and creativity. Hot Negative states can sometimes dissolve directly into Cool Positive ones, such as when a person who made us angry apologizes or a threat causing fear vanishes. Anger and worry can sometimes lose their energy and sink back into the Cool Negative arena of depression and defeat, which often happens when these emotions are not dealt with. And, finally, any sector of the Wheel can simply circle back on itself and persist, for days, months, or years.

The rest of this book is divided into four sections that correspond to the four parts of the Energy Wheel; each explores the types of spiritual practice best suited to its own energy. Depending on which energy best characterizes your work situation, or which one interests you most, you can turn to that section and start there. Each chapter within a section contains a general discussion of its topic—for example, anger—followed by a description of specific practices you can do, together with workplace examples. Remember, though, things will change. While this book is filled with specific practices and approaches for each energy state, its deeper goal is to help you learn how to navigate the whole Wheel, so wherever you find yourself, you have a sense of where you are and what to do.

Where we find ourselves on the Wheel is partly due to outward circumstances. But it is equally true that whether we are frustrated or exhilarated, bored or relaxed, angry or excited, stingy or generous depends on our attitude, our character, and our commitment to spiritual practice. The Wheel teaches us that no matter how stuck we may feel, we are never entirely trapped. There is always a way to move, to circulate, to alter the hue of the particular piece of colored popcorn where we have temporarily landed.

The Wheel, for better or worse, is our home. Whatever our situation at work, we are somewhere on the Wheel. The fundamental spiritual question the Wheel presents to us is: Does the Wheel turn us, or do we turn the Wheel?

As an experiment, as a journey, as an exploration, let's find out together what the Wheel has to teach us.

PRACTICES FOR THE ENERGY WHEEL

- What is your state of mind right now? What "color" are you?

- What was your state of mind four hours ago? What changed?

- Can you notice when your color changes? What happened? What caused the change?

part two

CONFLICT

HOW PLEASANT life would be if we never had to worry, if we never lost our temper, if we could always feel safe and secure! How satisfying our jobs would be if we could take it easy, work more slowly, and have enough time to do every task thoroughly and well. Unfortunately, anger, stress, worry, fear, and frustration—the negative, high-energy emotions of Conflict—are a part of both daily life and work life.

Recently I came across a survey that ranked different occupations by degree of stress. The occupation with the lowest stress was mandolin maker and one of those with the highest stress was taxi driver. I have already spoken of my high-stress experience in a taxi, and though I have never met a mandolin maker (are there really such people?), I once visited a violin repair shop. The sweet smell of wood shavings mingled with the odor of varnish as I waited while the owner patiently sanded the belly of a dismantled violin. "Be with you in a while," he explained as he bent over his tools, intent on his task. "Can't rush this." When was the last time you heard someone in the workplace say "Can't rush this"?

Those old-fashioned crafts jobs are a rarity these days. Stress is increasingly our on-the-job companion. If we want to be paid well, have good benefits, and keep climbing our career path, we must put up with a fast-paced, stressful work environment. There seems to be no help for it.

So what can we do?

First, we can recognize that when faced with stress, worry, and conflict, we are not helpless. Buddhism has an extensive body of spiritual practices for dealing with negative emotions, based on the recognition that they always arise for a reason. Beneath their chaos and confusion, such emotions as anger and fear have an underlying logic. If we understand the cause of anger, we are well on our way to neutralizing its destructive force.

For example, suppose your eight-year-old child came into the kitchen while you were washing the dishes, picked up one of the dishes you had just rinsed, and threw it against the wall. How would you react? You would be furious, of course. An eight-year-old child should never act in that way.

Now suppose your child had just been diagnosed with an inoperable brain tumor. How would you feel then? Of course, you would not feel angry at all. You would comfort the child, hold him in your arms, and do your best to calm him. He is not responsible. It is the tumor that is causing his outburst. You are not angry, not at all. Instead, you are terribly sad. You understand the cause of your child's actions.

When we understand the cause of a situation, the energy changes and begins to move in a different direction. All of the practices in this section have that goal—to help move the "negative" quality of Conflict into a positive, creative direction. I put the word *negative* in quotes because even the most painful emotion has its positive, constructive side. When we accidentally touch a hot stove, would we rather not feel the pain and let our hand be severely burned? The pain we feel is a warning, even a blessing, as it tries to protect us.

So it is with these painful emotions. Their job is to warn us, to rouse us, to help us to act and to move. Like the burning stove, the energy of Conflict is hot, but it is also true. Inside the coarse exterior of a coconut is sweet milk. Hidden within the rough outer shell of Conflict is the potential for growth, change, and deep nourishment.

In this section we will explore three forms of the energy of Conflict—stress, worry, and anger—and the spiritual practices that are suitable for each. And we conclude with a chapter on the forms of traditional meditation—sitting, standing, and walking—that are the basis for stress-related practices.

Have you ever watched carpenters build a house? They don't seem to move very fast. Their activity is a mixture of deliberate motions, such as carrying lumber, and quick, decisive ones, such as making a cut with a power saw. There is an optimum pace for every activity, as well there should be. Carpentry is an exacting skill. When a mistake is made, it takes far more time to repair the damage than it would take to do the job right

the first time. That is why, while the novice hurries, the master carpenter deliberates.

Office and service work, which make up the majority of jobs in our postindustrial economy, don't have the physical rhythm of crafts like carpentry. When we work at a desk, talk on the telephone, or stare at a computer screen, our pace is more mental, more jumpy and speedy. It is easy to get ahead of ourselves, to try to do too much at once. A carpenter who tried to work like that wouldn't last long. But in the service sector it is tempting to just keep moving faster and faster, in the false hope that more will get done. This was the fallacy of the rash of corporate layoffs in the early 1990s. A few years later, many of those same companies belatedly realized that ten people could not really do the work of fifteen. This

Plenty of time, plenty of care.

the self-mantra of Christine, a harried nurse

was small consolation for those ten people, the "lucky" ones who survived the purge, who were told they had to work harder and faster or else!

We may think that the pace of our work is something over which we have little control. But even in the most frenetic job, we can learn to cultivate and maintain an awareness of the body and breathing and establish small rituals of care in our movements—while walking down the hall, picking up the phone, or talking in a meeting. We can bring spiritual practice to bear in managing the speed and pace of our job.

Besides, stress is not always a negative thing. Sometimes stress is useful, as in the anxiety of an athlete before a big game. One element of managing stress is feeling in control. The athlete benefits from being pumped up before the game because she is confident she can excel. She is in control. The office worker who is asked to do ten hours' work in eight hours' time wilts under that stress because he knows there is no way he can perform well under those circumstances.

Stress, like any other portion of the Energy Wheel, can change and be transformed. For example, perhaps you are caught in a traffic jam on the way to an important meeting. Suddenly, you veer off the freeway and discover a back route. Thrilled with your solution, you drive like a maniac and get to your meeting just in time! You have transformed the negative stress of sitting in traffic into the creative stress of careening around curves.

Actually, the most common way to reduce stress on the job is to stop doing the job for a while. Taking a vacation or calling in sick is the fallback solution to ever-increasing job stress. No wonder more vacation time is such a sought-after benefit in worker contract negotiations!

Some people deal with stress by simply slowing down until the stress is manageable, regardless of the consequences to their career prospects. We see this in jobs where a worker goes through the motions, investing just enough energy to get by. That isn't an ideal solution, but sometimes it seems to be the only way to survive.

If stress is a problem for us at work, the least effective choice is to do nothing. Aside from its deleterious effects on our physical and mental well-being, stress has a way of boiling over at the least opportune time and wreaking havoc with our lives. We all need to find ways to manage stress, before stress manages us.

TRANSFORMING STRESS

Meet Christine, a registered nurse in a large urban hospital and a practicing Buddhist/Episcopalian. She loved nursing, but over the last few years her work had gotten much more difficult. The changes in healthcare and the rise of HMOs had forced her hospital, like many around the country, to make budget cuts and reduce staff. Christine now had many more patients to care for on her shift, and while some of her work had theoretically been shifted to less skilled workers, in reality Christine was still responsible. She was finding it harder and harder to actually care for people, which was what had attracted her to nursing in the first place. Some days she seriously considered leaving the profession.

"What's the most difficult part of your job?" I said.

"Not having enough time. No matter how much I try to arrange my work, there is never enough time to do the job right, and the patients constantly complain. I would too, if I were a patient. We just can't give the kind of care we used to."

"Is there any part of the day when you feel like you have more time?"

"We are supposed to have breaks, but many days we don't have time to take them."

I pictured in my mind the routine of the hospital where I had once been a patient. "What about walking down the halls? You must do a lot of walking."

"Running, is more like it." She laughed. "I try to be mindful of my breath, or my feet, as we do in meditation retreats, but there's usually too much on my mind, or I have to walk too fast."

"What about mantra walking?" I explained that this was a

practice of repeating a short sentence or phrase, one that fits with the rhythm of walking, as a way to focus and concentrate the mind. "How would you like to feel while you are walking?"

"I'd like to feel as though I had plenty of time!" Christine exclaimed, with a wry smile.

"Well, why not make that your mantra: 'plenty of time.'"

"How is that a mantra?" she asked. "I thought a mantra was some special sound."

I explained that I was using the word *mantra* in a more generic sense. There are indeed traditional mantras from the Hindu and Buddhist traditions that are like prayers. But just as you can compose your own prayer, you can develop your own mantra. Not every phrase is equally suitable. For example, the phrase "I *will* win the lottery," while an example of positive thinking, isn't the most spiritually deep sentiment. The most effective mantras are those that express core spiritual values—generosity, kindness, calm, and care.

I explained to Christine that she should recite her self-mantra silently in time with the movement of her feet, and Christine agreed to try it.

MAKING A SELF-MANTRA

Meditation teaches us how flexible time is and how much our sense of time is shaped by how we feel. When we are meditating, or are relaxed and enjoying ourselves, time seems to open up and stretch out. When that period ends we have a definite sense of "coming back" to ordinary or "clock" time. One method of dealing with stress is to open some space around clock time. A self-mantra tied to walking is one way to do that.

The next week, I asked Christine how the practice was going.

"It helped," she said, somewhat dubiously. "But it feels mechanical. After a while, I hardly pay attention to what I am saying. Besides, it isn't true. I don't have plenty of time."

"Maybe there needs to be something more in the words. What would really make you feel as though your job were going better?"

"If I were taking better care of the patients, giving them more attention."

"Could you change the mantra to include that?"

Christine thought about it for a while. "How about 'plenty of time, plenty of care'? That has a good rhythm."

That sounded good to me, so she agreed to try the mantra for another week and report back how it went.

The following week, Christine reported that the practice was working better. Putting the word *care* into the mantra seemed to make an important difference. She found she was walking a little slower, and when she entered a patient's room she felt a little more refreshed. But there was still a mechanical quality to the practice, something artificial. "I feel like I'm doing something to help," she said, "but I'm not sure how much it's helping."

I remembered when I was a hospital patient, how grateful I felt to the nurses for their smiles, their patience, their reassurance. "Thinking back," I said, "who comes to mind as your most memorable patient?"

"Oh, that would be Princess Juliana," Christine replied immediately. "She was a real princess, from some small European country. She was so gracious and charming. She always thanked me for everything I did, and told me stories about her life before the war. Once she said, 'You know, dear, I did some nursing during the war. The British took over my villa for an infirmary. You must remember, men think they run the world, but it's the women who really do. You have the most important job in the world. You must never forget that.'"

I suggested to Christine that, in addition to her mantra, she try to visualize the face of Princess Juliana.

"That's a lot to do," she said. "How can I visualize her face in addition to everything else?"

"Maybe not literally visualize," I said. "But see if you can remember the feeling you had when you were with her, and put that in your heart."

Christine reported back to me the following week that the practice seemed to be really working. Adding the "feeling" of Princess Juliana made all the difference.

"I feel like she is my guardian angel at work," she said. "I even say the mantra the way she would say it. 'Ple-e-e-enty of time! Ple-e-e-enty of care!' She was such a character."

"Do you think the mantra is helping you to feel less stressed?"

"I don't know," Christine replied. "My job is always going to be stressful. But I think I feel better about what I'm doing. At least I'm doing something about it."

Our bodies know when we have lost our sense of time and pace. We experience that loss in our pulse and blood pressure, even in the electrical conductivity of our skin. Can you notice when stress arises? For example:

- When you are in a meeting, try to notice the sensation of feeling that you need to say something. It will be slightly uncomfortable, like an itch or the need to sneeze. See if you can focus on the sensation for five or ten seconds before speaking. When you do speak, pay attention to how your voice feels in your body. Where do you feel it? In your throat, in your heart, in your stomach?

- When you are rushing to meet a deadline, or when you have to react to something beyond your control, such as a ringing phone, consciously adjust your pace. Force yourself to speed up until you can feel how fast you are going. Consciously slow down until the pace seems uncomfortably slow. Who is in control now?

LETTING THE PRACTICE GROW

Christine first reacted to the practice of mantra walking by seeing it as something artificial and mechanical. In some respects, it is. Many spiritual practices feel this way at first. It is important to realize that the practice itself is not as important as what opens within us as we do it. We are creatures of habit, and the sum of our habits is what keeps us from changing and growing. The practice is a gateway, a door to inner change. The great psychologist William James once remarked that most people are "set in plaster" by the time they are twenty-five or thirty. One purpose of spiritual practice is to melt that solid plaster, to make it soft and flexible again.

When doing a practice such as Christine did, it is natural to feel that not much is happening. But what do we expect to happen? Spiritual practice is not a quick fix like a cup of coffee. Success in spiritual work requires, among other qualities, patience and an alert, open mind. In Christine's case, she was honest enough to report that the practice wasn't really penetrating her inside. It was not until she thought of Princess Juliana and creatively adapted the practice to include a more inward, emotional element that the deeper practice emerged.

I saw Christine a few months later, and in the course of conversation asked her how her job was going and whether she was still doing the mantra walking. She confessed, a little sheepishly, that she was not.

"I kept it up for a while," she said. "But eventually I seemed to get tired of it. Every so often I try it again, though."

"And how are things going with your job?"

"Things are going better. I think doing the practice for that time really helped." She was silent for a moment. "You know, I didn't entirely stop doing the practice. It turned into something else. When I walk down the halls, I kind of hum inside my mind and try to keep a certain feeling in my heart. It's hard to describe, but it really seems to help. I feel like I'm managing the chaos, instead of letting it get to me."

I started to respond, but she interrupted me. "I just remembered something else. When a patient is really upset, when I go into the room now I make a point of sitting down. Sometimes the patient or family members are shouting or there is lots of upset and confusion. It's amazing how much I can calm things down just by sitting in a chair, even if I don't say anything."

"What made you think of that?" I said.

"It was Princess Juliana. Keeping her in my heart made me remember what she used to say when I came into her room. 'Sit down, dear. Sit down so I can look at you.' Of course, these days it's so unusual for a nurse or doctor to take the time to sit down, everybody is shocked. No wonder they calm down!"

This kind of development is exactly the sort of growth that the mantra-walking practice was designed to lead her to. Christine had taken what began as a gateway practice to a deeper level, one that she could continue to refine month after month, year after year. She had learned how to modulate the pace of her work life.

In bringing a spiritual practice to life, it is important to carry the effort lightly. It is all too easy to turn the effort into a kind of homework assignment or chore. The subject of the next story, George, was not exactly a victim of stress the way Christine was. Rather, he chose to work in such a way that he did not have to experience stress. This strategy helped him to cope, but it was keeping him from being successful as well as leading to Stagnation.

WORKING TOO SLOW

George, a Buddhist practitioner, worked in the warehouse in the company where I was once operations manager. George's job was to pack goods for shipment to customers. After George had worked there a few weeks, his boss came to me in frustration.

"Lew, you're a Buddhist. Could you talk to George? He's slow as molasses, and no matter what I say, I can't get him to work faster."

I wasn't sure if George's problem was that he was a Buddhist! But he and I had been to meditation retreats together. I invited him out for coffee and we had a talk. We spent some time talking about literature—George was an aspiring writer with a degree in English—and then the talk turned to work. George was concerned that his boss was not pleased with him, but he liked the work, because it allowed him to be mindful.

I asked him what he meant by mindful. "I try to work the way we do tasks during meditation retreat," he said. "I pay attention to what I am doing and concentrate on my breathing."

I had done some packing too, during the Christmas rush. I knew that the best packer, the one who made the fewest mistakes and packed the most boxes per hour, was a high school dropout named Johnny. He could laugh, talk, listen to the radio, fool around, and all the while his hands shaped the box, laid in the goods, wrapped the tape, sealed and stapled, without a miss. He rarely had to back up and do anything twice. Even in the way he laid down the stapler he had a strategy.

I suggested to George that he observe how Johnny packed boxes.

George resisted this advice. To him, Johnny was just a silly kid.

"Well," I replied, "he must be doing something right. Look at his scorecard." Each packer had a scorecard where his supervisor kept his packing rate and mistake log. Packers were paid extra for a good score.

George grudgingly agreed to do as I asked, and after a week we met again.

"All he does is listen to music and drink Coke," George complained.

"Maybe that's his way of staying relaxed," I suggested.

Cerebral people like George tend to use their experience of school and college as their model of how to learn something new. But the pace of work, particularly physical work, is more of a feeling than a thought. Speed is not always a matter of fast or slow. George was trying too hard to be careful and not make any mistakes and wasn't allowing the physical wisdom of his body to help. Johnny knew instinctively what many artists, athletes, and craftspeople carefully cultivate, a balance between paying attention and letting attention go. I once knew an artist who outdid Johnny by always keeping two radios going in his studio while he was painting. "Keeps my mind from getting in the way," he explained.

I was curious about George's problem so I found an excuse to go up to the warehouse and, under the pretext of talking to George's boss, stood where I could see both George and Johnny at work. Sure enough, George's movements were short and jerky. He looked as though he were carefully calculating every movement, trying to be "mindful," while Johnny, swaying to his radio sounds, didn't seem to be moving as fast as George, yet his package rack kept filling up.

It is not that Johnny is a model of spiritual practice, but his attitude can be a good lesson for those of us who are trying to do spiritual practice. Some part of him was alert and attentive, while another part was carefree and relaxed. He wanted the bonus that came from making few mistakes, but he also had an instinct for staying out of his own way. He may not have been highly educated, but in his manner of creatively managing stress and speed, he knew something.

PACE AND SPEED

Practicing with pace doesn't necessarily mean slowing down. In jobs like stock trader or police dispatcher, where rapid response is a job requirement, it might be more helpful to concentrate on the times in your day when the activity halts—when you take a break, get up from your chair, have lunch, walk to and from the bathroom. How are you spending that time? In your mind are you still back at your desk, staring at the console? Are you still rehearsing the words you should have said, the sale you could have gotten? That break time, in theory, belongs to you. You need to ask yourself, "How can I own this time? How can I make it mine?"

One principle that underlies many spiritual exercises is that the mind can concentrate on only one thing at a time. That is why the mantra is effective in mantra walking. That is why we visualize a word or a feeling in our heart. If we shift our attention to the part of ourselves that nourishes rather than drains us, even for a moment, the pressure of work will recede.

As we will discuss later in this section, just shifting our attention to the soles of our feet whenever we walk from place to place at work can have a marked effect on our state of mind. Stress forces our energy and attention up, into our head, where quick thinking helps us cope. Reversing that flow of energy downward, into our feet, where our body meets the ground, counteracts that tension in our head and neck. Besides, our feet can't think! Instead, they walk, they move and feel. The sensation of a rug or tile floor against the soles of our shoes can have a calming and healing quality. Like touching the tip of your finger to a piece of metal, that shift of energy to your feet can discharge all the electrical energy of your speed and stress, and, for a moment anyway, take you home.

PACE AND WORKING AT HOME

Speaking of home, the home office is where more and more people do their work. In my local area, a recent survey revealed that up to 15 percent of residences have some kind of home office in them. At home, we are theoretically in control. The challenge of practicing with speed and pace at home, where no one is imposing any particular pace on us, is to manage our supposed freedom. As anyone who has tried to work at home can testify, the home worker is tempted by all sorts of distractions.

Try to take fifteen minutes in the middle of the day, just before lunch. Turn off the phone, close the door, sit down in a chair or on a cushion, and be absolutely quiet, as discussed later in chapter 7. Your mind will be full of work thoughts. That is fine. Don't try to block them out. Just imagine them flowing through you, like the wind through the branches of a tree, and allow your mind to shift and sway as a tree would. Don't worry if you don't feel calm. How you feel isn't as important as what you do.

When you get up, see how slowly you can walk to the door. See how slowly you can open the door. See if you can retain the flavor or feeling of that lunchtime sitting during the rest of the day, just as Christine tried to keep the feeling of Princess Juliana with her during her rounds.

Remember: The goal is not to improve. The goal is to make the effort. Spiritual practice is like pouring water into a mountain of sand. The water disappears immediately, and there is little visible sign of the effort you have made. But over time, through repeated pouring and repeated efforts, the sand becomes more moist, more fresh, more workable.

Be willing to let the water disappear, and be willing to keep making the effort. A Buddhist teacher of old once said, "When you walk in the fog, little by little you become thoroughly wet." Be patient. The water will work its way through you.

PRACTICES FOR STRESS

- Whenever you sit down in a chair, take one breath. Whenever you get up, take one breath and shift your attention to your feet.

- When you walk through a doorway, pause slightly. Step in with your right foot.

- When you walk down a hall, try walking at 85 percent of your usual speed. Pay attention to the difference.

- When you type, try touching the keys more softly. Press them gently into the bed of the keyboard as though they were delicate like glass. Now go back to your old way of typing. What is the difference?

- Consider a phrase that expresses calm and care. Say it to yourself as you walk. Keep it short. If the phrase contracts or changes, let it change.

*I would like to beg you to have patience with every-
thing unresolved in your heart and to try to love the
questions themselves as if they were locked rooms or
books written in a very foreign language. Don't
search for the answers, which could not be given to
you now, because you would not be able to live them.
And the point is, to live everything. Live the questions now. Perhaps then, someday far in the future,
you will gradually, without even noticing it, live
your way into the answer.*

RAINER MARIA RILKE,
Letters to a Young Poet, translated by Stephen Mitchell

What am I going to do? What will I say?
Why is she out so late? Why hasn't
he called? What did I do wrong? What if I fail?
Suppose she dies?

These are examples of worry: compelling
questions that gnaw at our heart. Worry is the
mind's way of trying to deal with a fear, to explain it, verbalize it, define it, and organize it,
so the fear is not so shapeless and menacing.

Worry can be exhausting and destructive.
But it can also be creative. Which one it will be
depends on our attitude toward it and how we
use it. In the same sense that fear is courage in
the making, worry is wisdom in the making. It
seems to threaten us, but it is also trying to
help us.

As the owner of a start-up company
I worried a lot—about money, about the

product, about employees, about the clients, about the competition—and then about money again! I also worried about the individual tasks at hand—could I finish the new module in time, would the new system run fast enough, would the client send the check when he said he would?

These are the worries of a business owner. Employees have different, but equally distressing, worries. When we work for someone else, we worry about our ability to do the job, about the future of the company, about the unpredictability of our superiors, about conflicts with our colleagues, about money, and again about money. All of chapter 12 is devoted to money, but suffice it to say that money is the culprit lurking behind many workplace worries.

One of the pleasant parts about living in a monastery is that there are few worries. The whole environment is designed to minimize the kinds of stresses and distractions that we confront every day in the workplace. But in daily life, we worry a lot. Does this mean that anxiety and worry are somehow unspiritual? That worry is a sign of an insufficiently developed spiritual life?

I hope not! Worry is not a sign of spiritual weakness. It is an essential part of being human. While some kinds of worry are caused by pettiness and vanity, most worry comes from care for our livelihood, our family, our coworkers, our employees, our responsibilities as a mature adult.

When I would tell my Buddhist friends about my business worries, they would say, "Oh, why don't you practice more meditation, so you won't worry so much!" One said to me, "Worry is just a sensation! Why let it bother you?"

I understand that attitude, but I don't entirely agree with it. My experience taught me that worry is not a problem for which spiritual practice is an antidote; rather, worry itself can be a spiritual practice.

THE QUESTIONING SPIRIT

Worry manifests itself as a question. "Where am I going to find the money to meet next month's payroll?" "What will I do if I lose my job?" If we knew the answer to such questions we wouldn't be worrying! To worry is to be consumed by the question, to have the question echo in our mind until we would do anything to make it go away.

To seize on a question like this and work on it, over and over, is not unlike a certain kind of spiritual practice. Spiritual practice, at its root, is about asking fundamental questions: Who am I? Why am I here? What is my purpose? What if I get sick and die?

These are root worries. Regardless of whether our life is going well or badly, they are always there. In some sense, ordinary worry is a surface manifestation of root worry. One purpose of Buddhist practice is to learn how to deal with root worry. In that sense, any worry presents a good opportunity to raise the questioning spirit. The questioning spirit says, "I will stay with this question regardless of whether an answer ever comes. This question, for now, is my life."

WORKING WITH A QUESTION

Sometimes, in my workshops, I send people back to their jobs with the following assignment: Ask yourself, "What is the question?"

I don't explain it any more than that. I just say, "Find out what the question is."

Of all the practices that I have people do, this is the one they often find the most difficult. "What do you mean, 'Find out what the question is?' How am I supposed to know what the question is? Is this some kind of trick?"

It's interesting that the people who are resistant, who come back the following week with a blank look on their faces, are the ones whose jobs are going well. They are doing all right. Their questioning spirit isn't engaged. People who have a real problem at work typically know what the question is the minute they think about it. "What if the layoffs go through?" "How can I finish the project with no money in the budget?" "Why is my boss asking me to do the impossible?"

That's the gift that worry brings us. It lets us know what the question is. An eminent artist once said, "The great thing about being an artist is that for your whole life you know what your work is." I thought that was a wise observation. Many people never quite know what their focus should be. Worry helps. Worry lets us know what is important to us.

The practice of working with a question is not complicated. It involves the following four steps:

1. Raise the Question.

2. Repeat the Question.

3. Follow the Question.

4. Settle the Question.

The first two steps are fairly easy. "Raise the Question" means to construct a simple declarative sentence that states, as simply as possible, what the question is. Let's take one of those I mentioned earlier as an example: "What if the layoffs go through?"

Now, whenever it occurs to you, repeat that phrase to yourself. Just the simple exercise of verbalizing the question can have a significant impact. The worst kind of worry is the inarticulate kind. Giving shape to our fear, giving it verbal form, can help.

It is a little less obvious what "Follow the Question" means. It means remembering the question and bringing it repeatedly back into consciousness. It means breathing the question, walking the question, eating and sleeping the question—not obsessively, but attentively. One way to do this is to tie your recollection of the question to some specific action, such as standing up from your chair or opening your desk drawer. You can also work with a question using the mantra walking described in chapter 4. And if the question happens to recur in a somewhat different form—if, for example, the question "What if the layoffs go through?" rises back into your mind as "It would be a relief to know if the layoffs will go through"—then let it become the new question and follow it. Sometimes, in fact, the question changes into a statement. Often the question can get shorter, as it becomes more deep and familiar. It can even compress itself over time into a single word: "Layoffs!" Over time, the question takes on a life of its own. It moves under, around, and through your life, looking for a way through.

There are two ways to "Settle the Question." Either the question resolves itself into some kind of answer or else it subsides and dies away. If an answer comes, that's good! But if the question dies away, if over time you forget about it, that's all right too. Then the energy of the question gets put away, stored as though in a desk drawer, until the time comes for it to reemerge in another form.

How do we know the answer that comes is the "right" one? That too is a question, the next turn in the road down which the question has led us.

As a concrete example of this practice, meet Roberta, who actually solved a pressing workplace problem by engaging the questioning spirit.

TURNING ASIDE A THREAT

Roberta worked as the comptroller for an outdoor clothing manufacturer, managing the day-to-day financial operations. Formerly a bookkeeper, she had started going to night school to earn her accounting degree when her husband, a contractor, injured his back. Now she managed a staff of five people and was making more money than her husband. The company's founder, Nathan, had started the company with a few sewing machines in a backstreet warehouse. Now it was a thriving business, with a growing cachet among the mountain-climbing and river-rafting set. If the company had any structural problems, it was that it had outgrown Nathan's capacity to manage it. Like many charismatic founder-entrepreneurs, he insisted on making too many of the day-to-day decisions himself.

Nathan was also moody and capricious, but that did not affect Roberta too much. Nathan was not Roberta's boss. She reported to Steve, the senior vice president, an experienced business executive who managed the operational side of the company with all the professionalism that Nathan lacked.

One evening, Roberta was working late in her office when her intercom buzzed. To her surprise, it was Nathan. "Come to my office right away," he said brusquely. "I have something important to discuss."

Roberta complied, climbing the two flights of stairs to the executive offices with her notebook clutched nervously in her hand. She could not recall the last time she had been alone with Nathan in his office, and never after hours. She had no idea what he wanted.

As she entered Nathan's office, one look at his face told her that something was very wrong. She sat down with a sinking heart. Nathan wasted no time on pleasantries. "I want you to let Shirley go immediately. First thing tomorrow morning."

Shirley was the accounts receivable manager. Young, attractive, and single, she was the most popular person in Roberta's department. In fact, she and Roberta had become rather good friends and often ate lunch together. Roberta could not believe her ears.

"Why?" Roberta managed to blurt out. She could feel her heart pounding in her ears.

"Shirley's incompetent. She's rude to our vendors. I hear complaints about her all the time. If you had supervised her more closely I wouldn't have had to become involved."

Roberta started to interrupt and defend herself against this wholly unfair criticism, but Nathan ignored her. "I want you to draw up her termination papers first thing tomorrow morning and deliver them personally to me." He turned away to his computer screen and began typing, an abrupt dismissal.

During the drive home, Roberta was so upset she had to pull over to the side of the road. Her mind was racing as she struggled to absorb what had happened. She had heard that in the past Nathan had fired people without warning. She desperately wished that Steve had been there. Steve would have been professional and reasonable about this. That thought led to another, more troubling one. Why wasn't Steve the one to give her this news? Why had Nathan gone around Steve to speak her directly?

She didn't believe the reason Nathan had given her. Shirley's desk was close enough to hers for Roberta to overhear her phone conversations with vendors. If anything, Shirley was too polite. Roberta suspected a more sinister reason. Shirley was attractive, and Nathan had a reputation as a womanizer. Shirley had never said anything, but the previous week, while the two of them were out for a cup of coffee, Shirley had clearly been upset about something. Roberta was sure now she knew why.

What could she do? Her first thought was to call Steve. But what could she say? She had no proof of her suspicions. Besides, Steve was a man and was quite close to Nathan. As much as she liked and trusted Steve as a boss, in this case she was not sure what he would do. If Nathan could so abruptly fire Shirley, he could do the same to Roberta. Steve might not be able to protect her. He might, for reasons of his own, feel compelled to side with his boss, Nathan. Calling Steve might make things worse.

Suppose she went to Nathan in the morning and flatly refused to do what he asked? It wouldn't make any difference. He didn't need Roberta to fire Shirley, anyway. He could have Steve do it, or do it himself. And since that was true, why had he involved Roberta at all? To bend her to his will? Force her to become more of a "company woman"? Was she going to be the next target of Nathan's wandering eye, and if she resisted, would her fate be the same as Shirley's?

She was bursting to tell her husband, but tonight, of all nights, she dared not. He had called earlier in the day. His chronic back injury was not healing, and the latest round of X rays was not good. He was going to require surgery. He needed all of her support right now. Besides, her husband didn't like Nathan. He had worked for him as a contractor once and it had been a nightmare. With his hot temper, he would want to go down to the office and punch Nathan out.

She cooked dinner and went through the rest of the evening in a haze.

All she could think of, over and over again, was "What am I going to do?"

Roberta's dilemma had risks and dangers no matter what she did. She had to act, with little time to mull over her choices. A few years back, she had been to a meditation retreat I led. That night she called me, to ask my advice.

I told her I deeply sympathized but wasn't sure how much specific help I could give her. I didn't know enough about the people involved to recommend a course of action, and her dilemma raised possible legal issues that were beyond my competence. Instead we talked about the practice of Raising the Question. In her case, it wasn't difficult for her to form the question. "What am I going to do?" she said. "That's my question."

"Well then, stay with that. If you want, sit in the meditation posture and consciously repeat the question once a minute or so while you follow your breathing. See what happens." I encouraged her to have confidence in her own resources and judgment and to seek within herself for a decision she could live with by following the question until a possible solution presented itself.

"I'm doomed whatever I do," she said. But she agreed to try it.

When she called back, a few days later, I was relieved to discover that she had managed to defuse the situation in what seemed to me a most skillful way.

"I did what you said," Roberta told me, "and spent a couple of hours just sitting quietly, focusing on the question. I was pretty scared. I didn't have any experience dealing with something like this.

"It got a little boring just saying to myself 'What am I going to do?' over and over. For a while I just forgot about the question and followed my breathing, which helped with the fear. Then when the question came back into my mind, I realized it had changed. Now it was 'I know what I'm going to do.'

"At the same time, I thought of Alan. Alan is on our board. I had some financial papers in my briefcase that Alan needed to sign before he went on a trip abroad. I had been planning to send them to his house by courier in the morning, but instead I found myself getting up from my cushion, walking to the phone, and dialing his number. I held my breath while the phone rang, but finally he answered. I asked him if it would be all right for me to deliver the papers personally first thing the next morning and he said fine.

"So I left Nathan a voice mail that I would be late getting in because I had to take the papers over to Alan. My visit lasted all of a minute. Alan just signed the papers at the door and I left. I hung out at a coffee shop for another hour so I wouldn't get back to the office until about ten. I checked to make sure that Nathan was in his office and then went down to my desk and called him on the intercom. I told him that I was sorry that I was late, but Alan had invited me in and we had spent some time talking. Then I just let what I said hang in the air and waited to see what he would say.

"He didn't say anything. There was a long silence on the phone. Finally he just grunted and hung up.

"I waited a couple more days to see if anything else would come up about Shirley, but nothing did. Nathan never mentioned it again."

"What made you think of Alan?" I asked.

"I have no idea," Roberta replied. "It just popped into my head when I was meditating."

"Right when you changed the question?"

"I didn't change the question," Roberta said. "It changed itself."

Of course questions don't change themselves. Questioners do. When we ask ourselves a real, consequential question (as opposed to one like "Which necktie shall I wear today?"), our deeper resources are engaged. When we worry or are afraid, we think we are weak, but part of the energy of worry is to mobilize our strength and our power. Worry gives us power, if we are willing to trust it. I can't promise that every worry will be resolved as neatly as Roberta's was. The important point of Roberta's story is not so much that she found a way to sidestep her boss's threat, but that she went deep into herself to find that way. She used the question like a digging tool, to excavate something buried within her, a sense of strategy combined with some good luck to create a successful outcome.

WHAT IF WE AREN'T LUCKY?

Part of Roberta's success had to do with luck. It was lucky the powerful board member was home, for example. We think of luck as random, but from the Buddhist standpoint, it is not exactly so. Luck is partly about noticing, about paying attention to the various possibilities that swirl around us. Sometimes we can help to make our own luck—finding, among all the places to stand, a lucky spot. Roberta's story might be an example of that. And worry itself can sometimes help us to know in which direction to point our attention.

Things might have gone differently. Roberta might have decided that obeying her boss was her only realistic choice. The workplace is full of such moral compromises, and not every battle is worth risking our livelihood. Or, in the worst case, suppose she had refused to go along and was fired! Such examples of gross injustice do sometimes happen in the workplace. It may even have happened to you or someone you know. In these instances, legal action, more than spiritual practice, is often the answer. Today the newspapers are full of stories about sympathetic juries who order employers to pay damages to aggrieved workers. Some of these cases even find their way to the Supreme Court, which becomes the final arbiter, along with Congress, of such abuses. These extreme examples remind us of what I said at the beginning of this book: The workplace is an environment where power is unequally shared and sometimes abused. In part 5 we will devote an entire chapter to power—inner power, outer power, and the abuse and corruption of power.

Once at the end of a lecture at a Buddhist center, a woman asked me, "How do you work in the corporate world and hang on to your personal integrity?"

"I don't!" I reflexively responded.

"Oh, thank you!" she said, laughing. I think she was both surprised and relieved at my answer.

I was being a bit facile. I do try to hang on to as much of my personal integrity as I can, but I don't always succeed, and I am careful to pick and choose my battles. The arts of compromise and tactical retreat are as important as standing our ground. I learned a long time ago that there is no purity in the world of work, no black and white, only gray, and green, and yellow, and a whole palette of other colors.

To worry is to explore the palette, to work with every color in the rainbow, and to be enriched in the process.

PRACTICES FOR WORRY

- *Raise the Question.* If you can't quite figure out what the question is, begin with this one: "What am I worrying about?"

- *Repeat the Question.* Whenever it occurs to you, repeat the question to yourself. Don't expect an answer. Be prepared to ask the question forever. Try tying your recollection of the question to some physical action, such as getting up, sitting down, or walking. Repeat the question silently in rhythm with your walking.

- *Follow the Question.* Follow the question where it leads you. If the question changes, or if another question arises on its heels, go with that one.

- *Settle the Question.* If the practice of Raising the Question suggests an answer, you will be ready to go on to the next question, the next challenge. Even if it doesn't, one question leads to the next. The questioning spirit continues!

Anger at work is a big problem. For some people, it is the biggest problem.

Of course, the workplace is not the only part of our life where anger may arise. But the workplace is the prime locale where other people have real power over us—over our career and our livelihood. These people assess us, judge us, and command us. And besides our superiors, there are customers, vendors, competitors, and partners, all of whom can frustrate us, disappoint us, cheat us, or upset us.

This power imbalance can exaggerate the impact of workplace anger. Sometimes the mixture of powerlessness and anger can be dangerous, even fatal. We have all read the headlines about a disgruntled worker who takes a gun to work and opens fire.

Such cases are the consequence of workplace anger at its most extreme. For most of us anger at work is not so much an explosion as a long-simmering problem. Those who succumb to despair, alcohol and drug abuse, or even suicide don't make the headlines, but their victimization is equally tragic. If anger is a problem for us at work, then we must take it seriously. Even low-level anger, over a long period of time, is deleterious to our health, to our personal relationships, to our happiness, and certainly to our career.

The voice that says "Now I am angry" is not an angry voice but a true one.

Anger doesn't happen out of the blue. It usually arises because of a perceived injustice or unfairness. Even animals get angry, often for many of the same reasons we do. I once had a dog named Brahms, who was usually friendly and obedient. But if I scolded Brahms too harshly, he would hunker down and bare his fangs. He understood that I was the boss, and most of the time that was all right with him. But when Brahms felt I overstepped my bounds, when he felt I was abusing my power, he reacted. He got angry.

We humans are no different, although our anger is more complex than that of animals. There is often a large conceptual component in our anger. For example, a mere thought, a word or a phrase popping into our head, can make us furious. Animals don't have that problem. Also, we humans know better than to bare our fangs and growl at work. More typically, we conceal our anger or vent it privately to a trusted colleague, or to a friend or spouse after hours. Sometimes, our actual anger disguises itself as confusion, indecision, or even depression. In such cases, simply to understand that we are actually angry is a valuable insight! We also nurse and harbor our anger, sometimes for years. To forget about his anger all Brahms needed was a dog biscuit. Would that we humans forgave our adversaries so easily!

This chapter will explore more positive ways to handle anger. But more important, it will explore the potential of anger to contribute to inner growth. Precisely because anger is "hot," because its energy is so powerful, working with it as a spiritual practice can hone and temper our character in a way few other emotions can.

THE CAUSES OF ANGER

In a spiritual sense, we are ultimately responsible for our own anger. But it is a rare anger that is wholly unjustified. In fact, some anger is justified and appropriate. Anger arises from some mixture of external and internal causes, of justice and injustice, as well as our personal history of hurts and unresolved family battles.

It is tempting to leap immediately from experiencing anger to wanting to know its causes. Somehow we feel that if the "why" of anger can be known, then the "how" of dealing with it will be easier. The Buddhist approach to anger has a different emphasis. It does not ignore anger's causes, but it begins with the physical sensations of anger in our body. When we are all riled up, it is difficult to be objective about the causes of our anger. Putting some space and territory around our anger is a useful first step.

FEAR

Underlying most anger is its near cousin, fear. The physical sensations of fear and anger are quite similar—our heart races, our face flushes, our jaw and neck tighten. The main difference is that anger tends to urge us forward, to shout, to fight, to lash out, while fear urges us away, to run, to flee, to hide. Our deepest fear, of course, is the fear of dying, of being destroyed, of becoming nothing. To the extent that who we are is defined by our job, our work role, and our perceived status, anything that disturbs that identity can represent a serious threat. That is why a disgruntled worker might become so upset by a reprimand or a lost promotion that he would kill his colleagues and then himself. In that moment of rage and fear, to lose the job already feels like a death.

IS ANGER JUSTIFIABLE?

Anger invariably feels at least somewhat justified. When we are angry, we have the sense that it comes at us from outside, from something that someone did or said. That sense of injustice, of being wronged, is the fuel that keeps anger burning. As long as we feel that sense of being wronged, as long as we visualize ourselves as the victim, our anger will fan itself like a forest fire making its own wind.

And real injustice does occur in everyone's life everywhere in the world. Injustice fuels conflicts all over the planet, from the disagreements in families and companies, to the religious wars, ethnic conflicts, and terrorist attacks that cause so much suffering the world over. Whether the injustice involves a few people or an entire nation is not a matter of kind but only of degree.

In the workplace, anger comes in many flavors. Injustice is only one of many causes that conspire to produce anger. Here are a few examples.

ANGER OF THE VICTIM

Theodora was a middle manager in charge of a customer service group in the credit card department of a large bank. The bank was going through yet another round of layoffs, and one morning she arrived to find a memo from the executive suite in her in-basket directing her to reduce her staff by 20 percent while maintaining the same productivity goals on which her year-end bonus depended.

Naturally enough, she was furious. The directive was ill considered, poorly thought out, and uninformed about the conflicting pressures Theodora faced. It also threatened her earning power in a way she could not influence or control.

When Theodora described this situation to me, she acknowledged that she was very angry but felt uncomfortable with the feeling. She did not blame the executives on the top floor for her anger. She blamed herself for not being able to control her emotions better. Even though I assured her that it was not she but her superiors who were to blame, she could not shake the sense that her anger was a personal failing.

SUPPRESSED ANGER

In Theodora's case, she actually *felt* angry. But in a similar situation, some people experience not the hot feelings of anger but something close to the opposite—a loss of energy, a vague sense of annoyance, irritation, and confusion. This suppressed, dulled anger is as much anger as the hot kind, it has just taken a different and more indirect form. We all understand the dangerous consequences of expressing our anger directly at work, particularly to a superior. That danger sometimes causes us to censor our actual feeling, to the detriment of our mental and even physical health.

MISDIRECTED ANGER

James was a sales manager for a computer hardware manufacturer. He managed six other sales representatives who sold minicomputers to large corporations. One Friday, he got a call from one of his largest clients, who tersely informed him, with little explanation, that he was canceling a major purchase that James had thought was a sure thing.

Five minutes after receiving this call, Teresa, James's best sales rep, came into his office to ask if she could change the dates of her upcoming vacation.

"Why can't you make up your mind?" James snapped at her. "Don't you think I have anything better to do than juggle everyone's vacation calendar?"

We have all done this, redirected our anger at the nearest available target rather than the person with whom we are really angry. Again, power rules this scenario. As annoyed as James was at his inconsiderate customer, he couldn't get angry at him. James's livelihood depended on keeping his customers happy and the sales orders coming in. So Teresa was made to suffer.

The next day, once he had had a chance to calm down and reflect on what had happened, James explained the situation to Teresa and apologized. She was understanding—the whole sales group experienced similar pressures—but she also really appreciated James's apology.

EMBEDDED ANGER

George came to work with a scowl and left with a scowl. He was known around the office as the company grump. At meetings his responses were terse. On the phone, he dispensed with small talk.

Only his expertise as the department's most productive engineer redeemed him. George suffered from "embedded" anger. It was deep inside him. His anger probably had little to do with what was going on in the workplace. Perhaps his family life was unhappy. Perhaps he suffered from depression. Perhaps he was acting out angry feelings from an abusive childhood.

In all these examples, there appears to be some good reason for the anger, some justification. And that is what makes anger so complicated to deal with. The justification, as far as it goes, is unmistakably valid.

Even the Dalai Lama, whose patience and nonviolent compassion in the face of the invasion of his homeland won him the Nobel Peace Prize and the admiration of the world, acknowledges this point. In *Healing Anger,* he says:

> *If one has been treated very unfairly and if the situation is left unaddressed, it may have extremely negative consequences. . . . Such a situation calls for a strong counteraction. Under such circumstances, it is possible that one can, out of compassion for the perpetrator of the crime and without generating anger or hatred, actually take a strong stand and take strong countermeasures. In fact, one of the precepts of the [Buddhist] vows is to take strong countermeasures when the situation calls for it. If a Buddhist doesn't take strong countermeasures when the situation requires, then that constitutes an infraction of one of the vows.*

Essentially, the Dalai Lama is saying that when anger arises as a response to a true injustice, it is imperative, in a spiritual sense, to do something about it, to take "strong countermeasures." The problem is that the truth of the injustice by itself often helps to fuel the anger, to keep it from being transformed or resolved. Notice that the Dalai Lama emphasizes that when we take action against a real injustice, we must try to do so when we are not feeling angry. He also says that our motivation should be not so much to protect ourselves as to feel compassion for the perpetrator. This may seem to be spiritually a very advanced position, but I think all of us have the capacity to make efforts in this direction. Certainly, in the workplace, because of the power imbalance and the emphasis on money and profit, there are many small and not-so-small injustices. These occurrences, while they may cause much difficulty for us, are also opportunities to work on different ways to deal with anger.

THE VOICE OF TRUTH

From a spiritual perspective, the first step in dealing with our angry feelings is to actually feel our anger. When I tell people this, they are puzzled. Aren't we already doing that? they ask. When we are angry, of course, we feel angry!

But often this is not really so. Anger (or fear, for that matter) is such a powerful, hair-trigger emotion that there is often almost no space between feeling our anger and acting angry. Even when we do not act out our anger (and on the job we often have no choice but to suppress it!), we are swept up by it, immersed in it, engulfed by it. There is, in a spiritual sense, very little space or room around our anger. In fact, one of the reasons we typically "blow up" when we are angry is because we are unwilling to actually feel the anger. The sensations of anger are extremely unpleasant, and acting them out seems to provide some immediate relief.

How do we put space around our fear and anger? One way is through inner speech; for example, we say to ourselves, "Now I am angry." The voice that says "Now I am angry" is not an angry voice but a true one. This is what I call the Voice of Truth.

The more we are actually able to experience the unpleasant sensations of the anger—the churning stomach, the pounding heartbeat, the clenched jaw—the more there is some space around our anger, some envelope of patience. It helps if we can not only say the words to ourselves—"I am angry," or just "Angry!"—but actually *breathe* them. Even to breathe out the word "anger" two or three times while sitting in a chair, or to say it with every other step as we walk down the hall, can be powerfully transformative. In the workplace, there is usually no time for any extended kind of meditation. But any space is better than none, and the Voice of Truth, besides being a source of calm, can be a vehicle for gaining inner power.

And if our anger is the suppressed kind, if instead of feeling "hot" we feel "cold"—fatigued, irritated, or confused—then to reflect on this feeling and conclude "Wait! This is actually anger!" is another way the Voice of Truth can help give us inner power. And inner power, as we shall presently see, is an important key to the transformation of anger.

Let me tell you a true story of the power of the Voice of Truth, which was recounted to me by Michael, a police sergeant and Buddhist meditator.

I had just pulled a car over for a traffic violation. The license check showed that the car was stolen. When I got out of my car the suspect had already gotten out and was standing by the car with his arms folded. He was a large man, muscular and powerful. I did not see a weapon, but from the way he stood to face me, I could tell that he was not ready to give himself up. As soon as he spoke, he confirmed what I had already suspected, that he was a person with a prison record.

"I ain't goin'," the suspect said. "I ain't going back there."

For many years, until I started meditating, I was your typical gung-ho cop. I was a karate expert and knew many techniques to take a suspect down. But when this event happened I had been meditating for a few years, and I was experimenting with different ways to handle confrontations with a minimum of force.

"I understand that," I said, keeping my hands at my sides and not making any sudden moves. "But you've got to go. I have to take you in. That's my job."

The suspect shook his head from side to side, glaring at the ground. Then he looked up at me. "You afraid?"

I didn't have time to think about my response. "Yeah, I'm afraid," I said, which was the truth. This was a tense situation. I didn't know for sure if the suspect might have a concealed knife or gun. And he was physically strong enough to pose a threat even without a weapon. "I could get hurt," I said. "You could get hurt. But I don't think that's going to help things much, either way."

As soon as I said that I was afraid, something changed. The suspect relaxed a little. You see, he was a loser. He had nothing. His life was a mess. He was going back to jail for a long time. But he had one thing. He was big and strong, and he could hurt me. It was the truth. If I wasn't going to give him at least that, then it meant I didn't respect him for the one thing he had. It would be as though I didn't see him at all, and he truly had nothing to lose by fighting me. But when I said I was afraid, that meant something to him. It meant there was some measure of himself still worthy of respect.

"You ain't gonna handcuff me behind my back," he cried. "I can't stand that."

"All right," I said, moving slowly toward him, taking the handcuffs out. "You know I have to handcuff you. Those are the rules. But I'll do it in front."

The suspect let himself be handcuffed and got into my car without further incident.

I wanted to understand better what Michael had done. "Do you think in the old days, before you starting meditating, you would have admitted to the guy that you were afraid?"

"No way!" Michael laughed. "That would have been a show of weakness. I would have had my gun out before I got out of the car and had him spread-eagled on the hood before he had a chance to say or do anything."

"Don't you think you were taking a big chance by not having your weapon out when you got out of the car?"

Michael shrugged. "Being a policeman, you take chances every day. Violence leads to violence. If I'd come out with my gun it might have escalated the situation. I just chose the way that felt right for the situation. If I'd seen a weapon, I would have responded differently."

FEAR AND ANGER AS OPPORTUNITY

Many spiritually inclined people are ashamed of their angry feelings and see them as a kind of personal failure or shortcoming. They feel that if they were more spiritually developed, or better meditators, they would not be so angry. This is a laudable reflection on character. Because we know anger is not productive and that it can harm—both ourselves and others—we want to avoid that harm. But feeling ashamed of our anger doesn't really help. In fact, it often moves us in the direction of *not* feeling our anger, of not owning up to it.

After one of my classes a woman approached me. She had spent years agonizing over her angry feelings, which were intense and frequent, and was shocked and disturbed to hear me say that anger is energy, anger is human, and even that some forms of anger are justified and appropriate.

"I can't forgive myself," she said, beginning to cry. "I hurt so many people with my anger."

"If you don't forgive yourself," I replied, "then you will keep hurting people."

She heard what I said, but she was skeptical. She had grown up in a religious atmosphere where such feelings were sinful and wrong, something to be deeply ashamed of.

Fear and anger are not so much personal failings as a kind of potential wisdom. They express the truth of a situation. The police sergeant really was afraid. He had good reason to be too. He might have said, "I'm a cop. I'm tough. I shouldn't be afraid, and if I am I should never show it" but that is too full of "shoulds." Regardless of how we would like it to be, if we are angry, that is simply how it is.

This is a tricky point and one about which we need to be quite careful. I am definitely not saying that it is all right to throw our anger around like red paint. There is a big difference between feeling angry and acting angry, between experiencing anger's energy and releasing it carelessly. But whether our angry feelings are destructive or useful is entirely up to us. As someone who is hot-tempered and impatient by nature, I can say from my own experience that regardless of how justified our anger feels to us, it is usually not productive to express that anger at the moment we feel it. If we can put some space around that anger first and then say to our adversary, calmly, "I am very angry with you," that statement is charged with real inner strength, as when the police sergeant said, "Yeah, I'm afraid." Even though it may seem that blowing up at someone is a way to wield power, it is actually a sign of weakness. It usually makes things worse.

TRANSFORMING ANGER

Putting some space around our anger is the first step in transforming its energy into something more positive and constructive. Anger, being a hot energy, wants to move, to act, to be transformed and resolved. In the cases mentioned earlier, James's apology to his employee Teresa was an example of a transforming action. His anger and Teresa's hurt feelings both dissolved in his act of apology. And Theodora, the bank manager, was left hanging in a situation that she didn't see any way to resolve.

There are two types of spiritual practices that we can call on at this stage. One is to transform anger by raising up its antidotes—kindness, forgiveness, and compassion. The other is to deal with anger much as we did with worry in the previous chapter and practice Raising the Question.

RAISING THE ANTIDOTE

Anger seems to rise up as kind of protection for the self. There is a sense of wanting to claim territory, to say, in effect, "You can't do this to me! I am here!" In that sense, all anger, even the most justified, is self-righteous to some degree. Anger lifts the self up and gives it the high ground from which it can cry out, "Me! Me! Me!" It functions like the transmission in a car, automatically downshifting into overdrive on a steep hill. We feel that surge of power, that acceleration, as our anger propels itself forward with extra fuel.

This sense of justification is what makes anger so hard to deal with. There is nearly always some story to support the anger, some narrative that gives us a place to stand. In fact, when we listen to someone talk about his or her anger, what we usually hear is a convincing story line. The problem is that if it is *our* story line, if *we* are the ones feeling and expressing the anger, it is hard to know how much of the story line is really true and how much reflects our need for it to be true, even though it may not be.

Putting some space around our anger as I described earlier is a good first step, but by itself it is only a holding action. It doesn't really deal with the anger directly, it just widens the container. To really address the anger and to find out how much, or how little, of our sense of self-righteousness is warranted, we need to go further.

The antidotes to anger are, of course, kindness and generosity. Kindness exposes rather than protects the self. It calls out not "Me! Me! Me!" but "You! You! You!" Kindness ordinarily occurs when the self feels safe and secure. But it is possible to raise kindness even when the self feels endangered and exposed, even in the midst of anger.

THE PRACTICE OF THE HALF SMILE

Have you ever seen a picture or a statue of a Buddha with a frown? I don't think so, because nearly all Buddhas are shown with an enigmatic half smile. Not a broad grin, but a slight upraising of the lips. This is not just a matter of religious art, but a demonstration of a venerable Buddhist practice—the practice of the Half Smile.

When you are angry, perhaps in the midst of your practice of saying "Now I am angry," let your lips come up into a bit of a smile. It may be so subtle a smile that it is more an inner feeling than an expression anyone else can see. You may object, "I don't feel like smiling! I am angry. To smile would be dishonest!" Fine. Do it anyway. It won't be easy. Our anger doesn't want us to smile. In fact, that resistance is an interesting sensation. What are we afraid of? What harm would a bit of a smile do?

We tend to think that our facial expressions are effects of our feelings, but from the perspective of spiritual intention, the opposite is also true. Smiling, even when we don't feel like smiling, expresses our intention to open up a channel to kindness in the midst of our anger. A few years back, I read in a science journal about some research regarding facial expressions. The researchers wired people up to electrodes so they could measure their heartbeat, respiration, and galvanic skin response, the physiological markers for stress. Then they had the subjects look at, and then imitate, various facial expressions. Just adopting various expressions—from a friendly smile to a grimace of disgust—caused a physiological response, even though the subjects weren't necessarily "feeling" those emotions. Our facial muscles seem to be "wired" for feeling in both directions!

As a young Buddhist, I had a problem putting my hands together in the classic Buddhist greeting, which, in the monastery, we had to do constantly. Once I asked my teacher, "If I don't feel like putting my hands together, if I'm upset or angry, isn't that dishonest? How is my greeting then?" My teacher responded brusquely, "It is perfect!" It took me a long time to figure out what he meant. Finally I understood that the gesture and my momentary feeling each had its own distinct territory. Putting my hands together, regardless of how I felt about it, was an expression of respect complete in itself. It was, indeed, perfect.

The practice of the Half Smile is like that.

BREATHE!

Another antidote to anger is calm. But how can we be calm when we are angry? Conventional wisdom already knows the answer, as expressed in the phrases "Count to ten!" "Take a deep breath!" When we are angry, our breathing changes. It becomes tight, constricted, and high in the chest. Consciously breathing as though we were calm, releasing the muscles in our stomach and letting our breath fill our abdomen, helps us be more calm. Does our anger cause our tight breathing, or does our tight breathing make us feel angry? From the Buddhist standpoint, the two arise together. Changing one inevitably affects the other.

Incidentally, there is no way to practice this change of breathing in the abstract. The only way to learn it is actually to be angry! Sometimes, in my workshops, I ask people to close their eyes and think angry thoughts so that we can practice this change in breathing. Trying to make yourself angry is an interesting practice in itself. It allows you to see how much a thought, an image of another person, or a recollection of a cutting remark can trigger the whole constellation of angry feelings.

VISUALIZING OUR ADVERSARY IN KINDNESS

People often think of visualization as some exotic, complex practice. Some visualization practices are like that, but visualization can also be quite simple. In fact, it is something we do all the time. When we are angry, particularly when we are "harboring" anger—reviewing it in our mind long after the incident that made us angry has passed—we are probably engaged in a visualization of our adversary, conjuring up a mental image of our anger's object.

So when you are angry, close your eyes and imagine your adversary sitting before you in a chair. Feel your anger rising up, but suspend, if you can, the inner monologue that "speaks" the anger. Forget, for the moment, the put-downs and incisive comebacks that you wish you had said.

Instead, just focus on the feeling of your anger in your body and the image of your adversary before you. Yes, what she did made you angry. What she did was unfair, insensitive, even cruel.

Once you have the image of your adversary clearly in mind, imagine her doing or saying something quite unexpected. Imagine her performing an act of kindness. Imagine her apologizing to you or helping you. Imagine a steady stream of generosity and kindness flowing from your adversary to you.

How do you feel about your adversary now?

If you say, "That's ridiculous. She would never do that!" remember that this is *your* visualization, an act of focused, intentional imagination. Your imagined adversary can do whatever you intend for him or her to do.

Are you sure your resistance is really because you think your adversary would never be kind to you or because you don't want to give up the protective coating of your righteous anger, even for a moment?

This practice is like the Half Smile. Even though you don't feel like doing it, try to do it, just for a second or two.

What may happen in a practice like this is some further separation between our angry *feeling,* which is something we can affect through our own intention and practice, and the actual circumstance that makes us angry. The circumstance might indeed cry out for redress. But our feeling happens in its own space and time. The two are separate.

A vivid example of this from our own recent history was the civil rights movement, during which the whole nation saw the images of police dogs attacking unarmed people and hateful police officers beating crowds of praying demonstrators. How did the demonstrators feel about what was being done to them? Of course, they were angry. Who in their right mind would not be? But because the demonstrators were able, through their religious faith and training in nonviolence, to separate how they *felt* from what they actually *did,* they were the ones who prevailed, not their attackers. They took "strong countermeasures," in the Dalai Lama's words, but not from a position of violence and hate.

RAISING THE QUESTION

Suppose our workplace anger is truly justified, even though we have enveloped it with spaciousness and kindness. What should we do then?

At this point, our anger may have become less of a raw emotion and more of a clean, distilled energy. Yes, we think, we must do something about this. We can't just let the situation pass. We must take strong countermeasures. But now our anger is not tossing us around on its stormy sea. We have some clarity of purpose and of intent. The piece of our anger that was crying "Me! Me! Me!" has subsided somewhat. Now we are ready to say "I am still angry. I am clear about my part of the anger, but still a wrong was done. What should I do? How can I act from a place of confidence and strength in dealing with this situation?"

We explored the practice of raising and following such a question in our discussion of worry, and that same practice can be just as useful here. The same four steps apply:

1. Raise the Question.

2. Repeat the Question.

3. Follow the Question.

4. Settle the Question.

Your question could be "How shall I respond to this situation?" or "What is this anger asking me to do?" As you repeat such a question, returning to it as you get up or sit down, or as you are walking down the hall, you might gradually compress it into a word or two: "Response?" or "What to do?" You may find, as you keep returning your attention to the question, that your anger flares up, like embers in an old fire. See if you can redirect that energy back into raising the question. Your anger and your question are two halves of the same dilemma. And remember, the question may change unexpectedly. An answer may come. Or it may fade away. These are all valid and useful outcomes. There is no need to be critical of yourself if no immediate solution appears. Many workplace conflicts are intractable and difficult to solve. The effort will be valuable whether an answer comes or not.

This practice might be called the *strategic* component of anger, as the next example demonstrates.

CONFRONTING THE BOSS

David had a boss who seemed to take pleasure in demeaning people. It was not uncommon to see the boss in his office dressing down a subordinate over some supposed mistake. This made David quite angry. He felt bad for the people his boss mistreated (David, the boss's personal friend as well as an employee, was usually exempt from these outbursts) but didn't know what he could do about it. One day, he glanced into his boss's office as he was walking by and saw the familiar scene: The firm's sales director was being blamed for what was really the boss's own mistake. Immediately, David stepped into the office and physically placed himself between the boss and the sales director. "That's enough," he said to the boss.

The boss stared coldly at David. David just as coldly stared back. The sales director, sensing a chance to escape, excused himself and left.

"Don't ever do that again," the boss sputtered.

"That's what I was just going to say to you," David replied.

That was David's story.

"Whew!" I exclaimed when David recounted this story to me. "That was a risky thing to do. Were there any repercussions?"

"No," David explained. "I was lucky. My boss and I go way back. I had some immunity. Besides, I think at some level he really wanted someone to call him on that stuff. I just finally got clear enough in my own mind to do it."

"Were you angry?" I asked.

"Not when I was in there. Afterward I was a little shaky, though."

I would have been shaky too. In talking with David more, I realized that his ability to act that decisively was the result of a lot of prior work and processing of his anger, a lot of Raising the Question "What can I do here?" It may take weeks or months, but if the inner work is genuine and the intention is clear, when the moment to act presents itself, we will be ready.

PRACTICES FOR ANGER

- When you are angry, let the Voice of Truth say: "Now I am angry."

- Practice the Half Smile. Let your brow relax and feel the corners of your lips rise, almost invisibly, just enough for you to feel it.

- Breathe! Let your tight breath relax into your abdomen. Breathe slowly.

- Visualize your adversary performing an unexpected act of kindness.

- Raise the Question: "What is the source of this anger?" Allow various answers to pass through you.

- Raise the Question: "What can I do? How can I stand firm?"

- If your anger still suggests "strong countermeasures"—personal, administrative, or legal action—then try to take those actions from a place of confidence and strength.

This book would not be complete without a chapter on meditation. I have put it here, in the section on Conflict, rather than at the beginning of the book, because meditation is such an effective antidote to the negative emotions of Conflict. However, meditation also stands on its own as a fundamental spiritual practice whose benefits and purposes go far beyond symptomatic relief.

Meditation gets at the root of things. Why do we think and feel the way we do? Where

have we come from? Where are we going? What do we really want? These are the kinds of questions that meditation helps us explore. The purpose of meditation is to allow us to know ourselves more deeply, and by knowing ourselves, to know others as well. People who meditate regularly may not necessarily be luckier, wealthier, prettier, or more successful than people who don't, but they are likely to be deeper, more aware, and more complete.

One of the big changes in our society in the last thirty years is the acknowledgment of meditation as a normal, socially acceptable thing to do. When I first began Buddhist meditation in 1965, during my second year of college, it was quite exotic. In fact, the dean of my residence house summoned a friend of mine, also a meditator, to his office and said

All meditation has the same goal: to help you to know yourself more deeply, and by knowing yourself, to know others as well.

disapprovingly, "Jacob, I understand that you have *candles* in your room and that you *meditate!*" The conversation went downhill from there. Fortunately, there was no actual school rule against meditating, so all the dean could do was note with an icy gaze that candles were a fire hazard.

Times are different now, but when it comes to defining what meditation actually is, some confusion remains. Is it a technique? A way to achieve a certain state of mind? Is it about achieving some special insight? It can be all of these things. One common misconception is that meditation requires a special posture. But actually, it can be practiced in a variety of postures and circumstances. In her book *Living Meditation, Living Insight,* Dr. Thynn Thynn, a Burmese physician and Buddhist teacher, puts it this way:

> If meditation is to help you acquire peace of mind . . . then it must be a dynamic activity, part and parcel of your daily experience. Meditation is here and now, moment to moment, amid the ups and downs of life, amid conflicts, disappointments, and heartaches— amid success and stress.

In fact, there are scores of Buddhist meditation practices, each with its special emphasis and flavor. In addition to formal sitting meditation, there is walking meditation, standing meditation, meditation on sounds, visualization of colors and shapes, meditation on a repetitive word or phrase, meditation on the breath, and meditation on dying. People often think that meditation is unique to the traditions of Asia, but contemplative Christianity includes its own meditation practices. So do some traditions within Judaism and Islam. To stop doing what we ordinarily do and pay attention to our own mind and body is a universal spiritual activity.

In that broad sense, meditation is a way to make sense of our whole life, of our being born, of our living and our dying. Meditation is life itself.

When Shunryu Suzuki Roshi was diagnosed with terminal cancer, one of his doctors remarked, "But I thought Buddhist masters were beyond this sort of thing!" That idealistic misunderstanding was not uncommon thirty years ago. I hope that by now more people understand that meditation is not designed to make us superhuman, only more fully human. What distinguished my teacher's dying was not his disease but his attitude about it. From the time he was diagnosed to the time he died, his life appeared not to change one iota. He went about his ordinary routines, smiling and laughing as always. The fact that his dying was so ordinary was what made it so extraordinary. His example is still a resource to me thirty years later, a vivid demonstration of "profound ordinariness."

Profound ordinariness means seeing each detail of our everyday life as a gift—to truly live one day at a time. That is the power that a lifelong commitment to meditation can bring to us.

SITTING MEDITATION

All spiritual practice requires some ability to concentrate and pay attention, and there is no better way to cultivate that capacity than sitting quietly, doing nothing. Of course, to say "doing nothing" is an exaggeration. Even when we are sitting quite still, we are breathing, we are thinking, we are seeing and hearing and feeling. Quite a lot is going on. It would be more accurate to say "sitting quietly, doing nothing *else.*" Sitting meditation explores what goes on inside us when we stop doing all the other things we usually do.

It sounds simple, but if you have never tried it, it is not quite as easy as you think. And if you are already an experienced meditator, please read on. We're going to explore ways to practice meditation even in the midst of a busy workday.

THE NEUTRAL GEAR OF THE MIND

We think we know all about our mind. I am my mind—me, myself, and I. What's to know? Yet, in the course of the day, there is rarely an opportunity to stop and say, "What state of mind am I in right now?" In order to investigate our state of mind and know it more deeply, we need to let our mind slow down and experience itself at rest. We need to explore the neutral gear of our mind.

A car has a number of gears for moving forward and backward. But it also has a neutral gear, in which the engine is running, but the car isn't going anywhere. We don't usually sit in a car with the gears in neutral. But we could if we wanted to. Sitting quietly, doing nothing *else* is a way of letting the mind shift into neutral, to let its engine hum along without trying to go forward or backward, left or right. That way, we don't have to pay attention to where we are going, to the traffic around us, to the signals and lights. We can just pay attention to the car itself, to the steering wheel, the gear shift lever, and the hum of the engine.

HOW TO SIT

So let's try it now. Find a comfortable way to sit. If you want to sit on the floor, use a small cushion four to six inches tall. Cross your legs comfortably under you. If you sit in a chair, choose a chair that allows you to sit up reasonably straight. Avoid overstuffed armchairs. Try a director's chair or one of those classic wooden armchairs. The most important thing is to find a posture that will allow you to sit still, without fidgeting or shifting around, for at least ten or fifteen minutes.

At least some of the time, try sitting as you would at work. (Of course, if you are a carpenter or a flight attendant or have some other job where you rarely sit in a chair, see the sections later in this chapter on standing and walking meditation.) This advice especially applies to experienced meditators who are accustomed to the cross-legged sitting posture. The less our meditation relies on any particular posture, the more we can do it anywhere.

At work, try not to sit so formally that it disturbs others. When I was about nineteen, I had a job as a book-fetcher in a college library. Between fetches, I sat up straight on the fetcher's bench and tried to do meditation with my eyes closed. My boss, a prim, white-haired lady, must have thought I was quite strange. After three months, when my probation period was up, I was let go. I suppose that was my first lesson in spiritual practice at work!

Once you have found a comfortable, erect posture, let your hands rest comfortably in your lap or on your knees, palms up. What do you see? The potted plant across the room? The fire in the fireplace? Remember, we are trying to sit quietly and do *nothing* else, so let your gaze fall to the floor five to eight feet in front of you, but keep your eyes open. For beginners especially, meditating with your eyes closed can be distracting and quickly turn into another kind of *doing*.

Breathe naturally, and notice when you breathe in and breathe out.

This is both the same as ordinary breathing and different from it. We breathe all day and all night long. In fact, the typical person breathes about twenty thousand times a day. How many of them do we notice? Not very many.

So try noticing a few now. Try to keep track of the progress of your breath, feeling it come in and go out. You could try feeling the movement in your chest and stomach, in and out. Or you can concentrate on the feeling of air as it comes in and goes out through your nose.

See how long you can stay focused on breathing in and breathing out.

Did you lose track after two or three breaths and suddenly realize that you are thinking about your dentist's appointment tomorrow, or the fact that you forgot to put out the garbage for tomorrow morning's pickup?

Congratulations. You are normal. Besides, no one is keeping score.

It's not so easy to let the Chevrolet of our mind idle in neutral. The mind wants to be engaged, to be active, to do something. If you have ever watched monkeys in a zoo, they are always active, climbing here, jumping there, looking at this, grasping at that. That is the way our mind usually is, and there is nothing wrong with that. Your mind is like everything else about you, like your arms, your legs, your stomach, or your spleen. It is a gift, it has a function, and without it we would not be human. We should be grateful for our busy mind.

Nevertheless, to be busy is not the only function of the mind. The mind can also be concentrated, reflective, and self-aware. In fact, that is the natural resting state of the mind, its neutral gear. What's even more important, in neutral gear we can take charge of our state of mind.

THOUGHTS AND THINKING

One of the questions most commonly asked by beginning meditators is "What shall I do about my thoughts?" The simple answer is: Nothing! Thoughts are a normal function of the mind, rising and falling like the waves on the surface of the ocean. With more experience, we may find that there are periods during our meditation when thoughts are few and our mind is calm and serene. Other times, our mind will be congested with an endless stream of thoughts. The main thing is not to seize onto any thought and gnaw on it the way a dog chews a bone. Let thoughts come in, and let them go out. If we don't seize on them, they won't stay long. They become like dinner guests who have outstayed their welcome. If we don't engage them in conversation, before long they will take the hint and find their way to the door.

STANDING MEDITATION

So having tried sitting, let's try standing. Stand naturally, with your legs about shoulder's width apart, your weight settled comfortably in the middle of your feet, and your hands hanging naturally a little away from your sides.

Now, just stand there.

After a few moments, it may seem a bit strange.

Keep standing. Notice your breathing. Be aware of your body. Feel the soles of your feet and the ground beneath them.

Can you continue noticing your breath while you stand? How does it feel? Is it different from when you are sitting down? Do you have an easier time keeping track of the breath, or harder? What are your eyes doing? Do you have more of a tendency to look around?

How is this different from standing in the checkout line, or standing watching a sunset, or standing at the water cooler at work, or standing in the snack kitchen, waiting for the water to boil?

That is the point. Meditation is not some mysterious, *other* thing that we need to learn to do, like playing golf or studying calculus. It is something that we are already almost doing. How often, in the course of the workday, do you find yourself just standing? Waiting? What is the difference between that ordinary standing and this so-called meditation standing?

EVERYONE HAS SAT!

That question reminds me of a story from my early days as a Buddhist student. During the 1960s, many unusual people showed up at the monastery gate. Among them was a young electrician from Sweden, whose limited command of English was further hindered by a few beers.

He was met at the gate by the director, who asked him what he wanted.

"I want to study Buddhism!" the Swede bellowed.

"Have you ever sat?" the director asked, using our shorthand expression for "Have you ever done sitting meditation?"

The Swede didn't know how to answer this question. It seemed to be a question in plain English, and he understood the words, but somehow the meaning eluded him. Was this some kind of Buddhist trick? Was the director making fun of him? Of course he had sat.

Finally, he decided that if the question was a trick he would not take the bait. He drew himself up to his full height and shouted, "Everyone has sat!"

The Swede entered the retreat center and remained there for

several years. He was right, of course. All people have sat. We do it every day. We stand too, and walk, and lie down.

WALKING MEDITATION

Buddhism speaks of the "four postures"—walking, standing, sitting, and lying down. I don't know what kind of job you do, but I know that during the day sometime, somewhere, you sit, walk, and stand. (The fourth posture, lying down, is probably not part of your workday, unless you are a car mechanic or a subject in a sleep research lab!) You may walk down the hall to the copy machine, from your truck to the job site, or down a hospital hallway or school corridor. At most jobs, walking is transition time, an in-between activity. As such, it is a perfect opportunity to capture a few moments for meditation.

Here's how it is traditionally done. First, make a fist with your left hand, with the thumb inside, and put your right hand over it, with its thumb on top. Now rest your clasped hands lightly against your chest, just below the breastbone. Imagine that you are holding on to an imaginary pole, like a merry-go-round pole. As you move forward, imagine the pole moving along with you. If you find it more comfortable to just loosely clasp your hands on your chest or let them hang naturally at your side, that is fine too.

Now take a step, and as you do, exhale. As you inhale, take another step. Exhale, another step. One step, one breath. You will start gliding along at about half your normal walking pace but with your body in balance, aligned with your merry-go-round pole. What's more, you can continue the practice of noticing your breaths just as you were doing while sitting. Think of this walking meditation as a way of moving your sitting posture slowly and smoothly through time and space.

You probably can't walk that slowly at work, at least not without attracting puzzled glances. At work, walk at your normal pace, but keep your attention in the soles of the feet. That simple effort, which shifts your attention away from the thoughts in your head down to the place where your feet touch the earth, will have a marked effect on your state of mind.

Another way to meditate while walking at normal speed is to try saying silently to yourself, every third or fourth step, the word *walking*.

"Walking."

"Walking."

"Walking."

We have met this voice before. Remember Michael, the police sergeant, and the Voice of Truth? The voice saying "walking" is also the Voice of Truth. The word *walking* indisputably describes what you are doing. If you are in an upset, distracted, or angry state of mind, this interior truth-telling has a curious power to help you as you move through time and space, keeping time with a word.

This is a practice you can do anywhere. No one need know. Are you on the way to the snack kitchen to grab a cup of coffee? Is your mind swirling with the phone calls you have to make, the memos you have to write, the unfinished work stacking up on your desk?

Fine. That will all be there when you get back. In the meantime: "Walking. Walking. Walking."

Say it going, and say it coming back with your steaming cup balanced in your hand. Using your mind like this may seem to be a waste of time, but it is not. It is developing the capacity of your mind to be present with itself.

SITTING MEDITATION AT WORK

"Everyone has sat!" If you have a sit-down job, then sitting is part of what you do at work. Trying to liberate time for sitting meditation at work is a little more problematical than walking. When you are walking around, you are usually between work activities. But when you are sitting, you are supposed to be working! I don't want this book to be responsible for your boss coming up to you with a scowl like my old college dean's and saying, "I hear you have been *meditating* at work!" (I also want to acknowledge the growing number of managers who are sympathetic to meditation and may have even tried it themselves. The workplace is changing as I write.)

If you have a job like data entry, where you are supposed to be continuously productive all the time you are sitting at your desk, then you will have to find "sitting moments" on your breaks. But if your work is more project oriented—if you are a manager, for example, or a computer programmer—then some time for planning and reflection is part of what you are paid to do.

Some productivity experts encourage deskbound workers to look away from their work now and again, as an antidote to eyestrain and bad posture. These sitting breaks are a perfect time for a one-minute period of sitting meditation. Remember my experience as a book-fetcher and try not to *look* like you are meditating. But you can do two things, both of which are relatively inconspicuous: First, put both feet flat on the floor, and second, let your hands rest comfortably in your lap or on your armrests.

Try doing one cycle of ten breaths. That should take about a minute. Try it once an hour or so, eight times in the course of the day.

If you work in front of a computer screen, focus your eyes on the monitor case an inch or so below the bottom of the screen. Often the maker's label is displayed there. You might want to tape a rectangle of colored paper on that spot. That can be your "breath" paper. Whenever you look at it, it reminds you to breathe. Another tactic is to turn the computer monitor (the screen) off for a few moments. Many people don't realize you can power the monitor off and on without having any effect on the computer itself. You might find it relaxing, even liberating, to contemplate that blank screen for a few moments as you breathe. When you are looking at the paper rectangle or the blank screen, you are not working, you are not thinking, you are not angry or distracted or bored or stressed out or whatever you are for the rest of the day.

You are breathing.

You are noticing that you are breathing.

For a moment, you have stepped outside the "white circle" of your customary activity.

Have you ever watched a wrestling match? The wrestlers must remain within a white circle or else they are penalized. If they leave the circle too often, they are disqualified. Those are the rules of wrestling.

The "wrestling circle" of our mind—its size, its shape, its location and domain—belongs to us. We can draw the circle where we want.

It's our circle.

One minute an hour, eight times a day, let the circle widen and change. It will snap nearly back into its old shape the minute you take your hands off the armrests and your eyes off the rectangle of colored paper or the blank screen. But something will have changed.

The circle will have become one minute more flexible, one minute softer, one minute more within your care and awareness.

The wrestling circle belongs entirely to you.

PRACTICES FOR MEDITATION

- Once an hour, sit for one minute and follow your breathing in and out.

- While standing, put your attention in your feet. Feel the earth.

- While walking, attend to your walking with the Voice of Truth, saying "Walking, Walking."

- Ask yourself, "What state of mind am I in right now?" Whatever the answer may be—"distracted," "peaceful," "angry"—is the Voice of Truth. It is you.

part three

STAGNATION

STAGNATION is the section of the Energy Wheel that includes depression, sadness, discouragement, and boredom. Stagnation states are characterized by an inability to move, to change, to develop, to grow. Common workplace examples are a lack of commitment to the job, an inability to improve it, or a reluctance to seek a different job. There is a gluelike quality to this territory, a sense of lethargy and fatigue. We languish in Stagnation in response to a difficulty that we cannot solve or overcome.

Stagnation is a low-energy state, cool rather than hot. It is the opposite of Conflict. In Conflict we feel strongly our anger, worry, and stress. We fight for the promotion, confront the boss, try to make the job interesting. Even though conflict is unpleasant, our energy is mobilized. But in Stagnation, we lose our energy and drop back, like a snail trying to crawl out of a well and slipping back down. This condition feels like a dead end, a failure, a defeat. And unless we can find a way to pick ourselves up and try again, we may indeed be defeated.

What redeems Stagnation is that it also is a place, like a womb or swamp, where new life can form. A swamp teems with life. Because it is quiet and protected, fragile creatures like tadpoles are safe there. The marshland of Stagnation provides a safe haven to which we can retreat when we are wounded.

In Stagnation we don't want to get up in the morning. We dawdle on the job; we don't put our all into it. The work we do pays the rent, but it isn't satisfying. In Stagnation it is not so much that we feel bad as that we have lost track of how we feel. When someone asks us how we feel about our job, we may just shrug. In that situation, even to feel *bad* might be an improvement!

The practices we explore in this section are all methods to light our fire, to get us moving, to help us find something interesting to do, even if it is as simple as listening to the wind or watering a plant. Ultimately, it is not our job that is blue, it is ourselves. Our job may not be something we can change. But how we feel about it, and the kind of energy we bring to it, is indeed something we can change. That is the spiritual opportunity of Stagnation.

We must remember, though, that to climb up out of the swamp is to return to the problems and conflicts that made us retreat there in the first place. In other words, we must be prepared to trade safety for energy and to return to the arena of stress and conflict—this time, we hope, better prepared. The goal of these practices is not necessarily to feel better but simply to feel *something*. For a while, we may actually feel worse. But we will feel more deeply, and by following that feeling, we can emerge stronger, clearer, and more confident.

WHAT IS BORING?

Boredom is a fairly common workplace complaint. There are numerous jobs (housecleaning, factory work, receptionist, retail clerk) that many people would consider boring. In fact, fifty years ago, that's the way most work was. To have an interesting, challenging job is one of the privileges of living in an affluent society. On the other hand, some people—artists and writers, for example—may prefer boring day jobs be-

cause they don't draw psychic and creative energy away from their primary vocation.

But when we say something is boring, what do we really mean? During her years as a kindergarten teacher, my wife would often hear her students complain, "I'm bored!" Or she would hear from a parent, "My Jennifer is not being challenged in the classroom. She's bored!" In most cases, all this meant was that Jennifer would rather be doing something else and didn't want to invest herself in the activity at hand. We all feel that way from time to time.

When we are bored at work, it may mean that our job is intrinsically uninteresting. Or it may also mean that regardless of the merit of our work, we have made a conscious decision to shut ourselves off from what is actually going on.

Howdy, big spender!

daily greeting of the
Existential Toll-taker

Right after graduating from college, my wife and I shared a house with another couple, one of whom worked as a checkout clerk at the local supermarket. He aspired to be a social worker and found the interactions with customers, his coworkers, and the store managers fascinating. To him, it was all a real-life education. The other checkout clerks, apparently, did not share his enthusiasm. To them it was just a drudge job.

Clearly, what is a boring job to one person may be fascinating to another. So as we begin our exploration of boredom, let's consider one part of the workday that almost everyone would agree is fairly uninteresting—the commute.

TIME, SPEED, AND TRAVEL

How long is your commute? (If you work at home, please don't gloat when you answer this question!) If you are the average American, your commute is forty minutes each way. Nearly an hour and a half of your life, five days a week, forty-nine weeks a year, year in and year out. If we add up all that time in the course of a forty-five-year work life it comes to 16,538 hours. That's 689 days, or nearly two full years!

Two years of our life, to and from work. That's a lot of time. How do we use it? If we are like the typical commuter, we may fill up the time listening to music or the radio, or else thinking about work. Or we may talk on our cell phones or listen to books on tape. Thirty years ago, Suzuki Roshi was astonished to discover that Americans liked to read in bed! To him that was already doing too many things at once. I can only imagine what he would have thought of people talking on their cell phones while driving. One way or another, we fill up the time as we speed along, anxious to get to work in the morning or to get home in the evening. We are on the move, both physically and mentally.

The modern world has radically changed our sense of time. Until the invention of the railroad, no one could imagine traveling faster than the speed of a galloping horse. The speed with which we race around today does more than add complexity to our day. It changes the very nature of our perceptions. *The Farther Shore: A Natural History of Perception,* by Dr. Don Gifford, explores the impact of modern life on perception, especially how the speed of movement has profoundly altered the way we see the world. Here are his comments about the distance between Williamstown, New York, and New York City:

> If we traveled that distance on horseback, the city would be three and a half or four days away (thirty-six times "farther" than it is by car); on foot ten days away. At first, we might imagine the walk or the ride as a marathon of monotony and impatience. But that could hardly have been the case when one was in the midst of it. One must have settled into a rhythm, the mind and eye busy with a passing scene rich in complex detail unavailable to us in our glass and steel cocoons at sixty miles per hour.

What Professor Gifford is saying is that the slower we travel, the more we see and the less bored we are. It seems as though speed should add quality and variety to our life, but the opposite is true. Driving a car or sitting in a bus or train as we travel to work shuts us off from our actual experience. When we drive, our attention is on the road and the other speeding cars. On the bus or train, we are crowded together in a noisy, often unpleasant environment. We seem to be sitting still, but the experience is far from quiet. And because our environment is speedy and distracted, so is our mind.

Yet regardless of how little autonomy we have when we are actually at work, the time we spend commuting is completely our own. We aren't yet on the job, or we have already left it. No one is there to tell us what to do. That is why commuting time is a good opportunity to introduce some spiritual practice into our workday.

LISTENING WITHOUT JUDGMENT

An hour and twenty minutes, coming and going, with nothing to do. Why not experiment? Have you ever tried driving five miles an hour slower than you usually do? Staying in the same lane behind a slow car? Paying attention to the sounds around you, the hum of the engine, the clickety-clack of the train tracks, the rush and clamor of surrounding traffic? Can we tune in to the unexpurgated reality all around us? And if you are one of those lucky souls who walk to work (Yes, some people still do!), then you are way ahead of the drivers and train travelers. You actually have scenery—sights, smells, and sounds—to enjoy.

If you are accustomed to listening to the radio or letting your mind wander with thoughts of work, I encourage you to give up some of these distractions and instead awaken the senses by listening to the sounds all around you—the roar of traffic, the wind rushing by, the hum of conversation on the bus or train. Just listen without making any judgments, without giving in to impatience and boredom, without reaching for the newspaper and the radio. Pretend you are one of Professor Gifford's carriage travelers, engrossed in the ever-changing panorama of sight and sound as you move along.

This exercise is really two practices in one. It is a practice of pure listening as well as a practice of suspending judgment. How much of our workday is involved in making judgments? Perhaps critical judgment is the main skill you are paid for! This product is good, we say, that one is bad. This person did a good job, that one needs improvement. This client is worth pursuing, that one is a loser. What do our colleagues talk about at lunch? How much of it is criticizing, carping, gossip? The whole workplace teems with judgment. No wonder it is so stressful!

See if you can spend even ten minutes on your way to or from work just listening without making any judgments at all, without honking back when someone honks at you, without turning on the radio to block it all out. If you read the paper on the train, try folding it up. If you are one of those people whose briefcase is open the minute you board the bus, leave it closed. You have another job to do just now, the practice of pure listening.

When is the last time you actually took time to pay attention to the sounds of the world? Perhaps when you took a walk in a park and could hear the songbirds chirping in the trees. How did you feel? Did it lift your spirits? Perhaps you do not think that listening to the sounds of traffic or the rushing of wind along the freeway is terribly inspiring. But the sound itself doesn't know whether it is pleasant or unpleasant. It just sounds off, without embarrassment or fear of criticism. If your blood boils when someone cuts in front of you and leans on the horn, it's not the horn's fault. The honking horn is just a sound, flowing in, flowing out. We are the ones who assign it a label: BAD! What does it cost us to practice giving up that BAD! and seeing what symphony is being played all around us when we suspend judgment and just listen?

The composer John Cage used to stage performance pieces in which he would walk on stage, turn on three, ten, or twenty radios to different stations, and let them play. When he first did this many years ago, concertgoers were irritated, then bemused. Was this music? Was it noise? What was it? Mr. Cage was an avid student of Buddhism. He understood that pure sound, regardless of its content, can be a joy, and the listener, not the sound, is the one who determines whether to let the joy in.

Whether we listen with criticism and judgment is not something that happens inside the ears but between them. It is a manner of adjusting our inner tuning knob to listen not to the meaning of the sound (such as the words of our irritating coworker or carpool partner) but to the sound itself.

DRIVER SEEING

Recently, when I was describing the practice of Listening Without Judgment to a group of Buddhists, a man named Peter raised his hand. "I have a car practice too," he said. "What I try to do is make eye contact with the other driver whenever I can. It is so easy to forget that the person in the other car is a human being and not just a vehicle."

"How well does that work?" I asked. "Isn't it hard to catch their eye?"

"You'd be surprised," he replied. "It's almost as though people are waiting for you to see them. A lot of times they wave, and I wave back. It really makes a difference."

I appreciated this lesson in Driver Seeing and began to practice it myself. Peter was right. It is one thing to casually wave when someone acts courteously to you while driving. It is a more consequential effort to actually make eye contact, to really see the other person behind the wheel.

When I brought this suggestion up in other workshops, people pointed out a connection between their workplace environment and driving on the highway. Our car surrounds us with a hard shell. That shell separates us from other drivers and has a subtle dehumanizing effect. This can lead to behavior we wouldn't dream of in other circumstances, from curses and gestures to true physical violence. Road rage is becoming so common that some psychologists are making it their specialty. At work, we have a shell too, a psychological rather than physical one. On the job, we are not just Joe or Sally, we are the boss, the assistant, the doctor or nurse, the teacher or principal.

The practices of Listening Without Judgment and Driver Seeing are two ways to become more aware of the shell and to reach out beyond it. If they can work on the highway, perhaps they might help on the job too. To understand that the shell is a common choice we have all made might allow us to view our coworkers with more transparency and more heart.

NOT CHANGING LANES

While I was commuting across the Golden Gate Bridge to San Francisco every day, I would notice how frequently people (including me!) changed lanes to get into what seemed to be the fastest lane at the moment. The bridge, built sixty years ago, is only six lanes across for both directions of traffic, so it would often get clogged. A hyperintelligent seagull, looking down on the scene from the top of the bridge, might observe what we down in our cars could not—that all that lane-changing activity was just slowing everybody down. If everybody would just stay put, they would get where they were going faster. But that can only happen if every driver, on his or her own, makes the same decision. So, as illogical as it often seemed, I experimented with forcing myself to stay in the lane I was in. I can't say if the seagull was always right (sometimes a car stalls and one lane gets completely blocked!). But I felt more relaxed. I didn't have to worry about shifting this way or that, I just followed the car in front of me. And when people tried to cut in front of me, I let them. I had the feeling that if I let someone in today, someone else might let me in tomorrow.

We are always part of the larger situation, whether we are on the freeway or in the middle of our workday. What might seem to work best for us at the moment might not work best for the whole situation. Even though we know that our solitary decision will not magically alter the behavior of all the other drivers, staying in our own lane is not just naive altruism. It is more like making a spiritual investment and a connection with something larger than ourselves, not because it will reap an immediate reward but because it alters the chemistry between us and our surroundings in an intriguing and calming way.

BOREDOM AND HUMOR

There was one toll-taker who met every car with a cheery grin and the greeting "Howdy, big spender!" as he took our two dollars. He didn't just do it occasionally. Invariably, when I drove through his booth, his greeting and his smile were the same. I found myself looking ahead as I approached the toll plaza, to see if I could move into his lane. Once I joined in by saying "What makes you think I'm a big spender?"

"I can see it in your eyes," he replied, raising and lowering his eyebrows like Groucho Marx. That greeting was his way of getting through the day, using humor to enliven his repetitive job. Since of course we all paid the same two dollars, there was something about the way he greeted me every day as a "big spender" that made me feel a bit better about myself. I still remember that feeling now, many years later.

Few people pick a boring job by choice. Either their real vocation lies somewhere else, or their circumstances don't allow them to change or quit. The daughter of a good friend once cracked up the judges at her tryout for the Yale School of Drama by answering the question "Why do you want to be an actress?" with "Oh, I'm sorry. I thought I was trying out to be a waitress!"

The usual thinking about such a job is "I don't mind how boring it is. It's not what I'm *really* doing. I don't have to invest any emotional energy in it. If all goes well, I won't be doing it for long." That's a good rationale, but these boring, pay-the-rent jobs have a way of lasting longer than we expected.

"Howdy, big spender!" This tag line has more in it than meets the eye. It says, "I'm not going to just do the job. I'm going to create the job." It expresses a clear intention to reach out past the limits of the job description with laughter and good humor. How many toll-takers do you know who have the energy and perseverance to do that? Most of them don't say anything, they just take our money. I can think of many jobs where this kind of approach could be effective— waitress, retail clerk, customer service representative, bartender, taxi or bus driver.

Is "Howdy, big spender!" a spiritual practice? Done once or twice, it's just a funny remark. But to keep it up, day after day, the way he did, with that cheery grin on his face, is much more than humor. The Existential Toll-taker was giving something of himself to each driver who passed through and engaging the world at a spiritual rather than material level.

DOING THE JOB, CREATING THE JOB

As another example, I would like to introduce you to the woman I call the World's Greatest Receptionist. I have great sympathy for office receptionists. Theirs is a difficult job, and one that often commands little respect. But they are the face and voice of the whole company. Whenever I am visiting a prospective client for the first time, I make it a point to spend time with the receptionist. I find that I often learn more about what the company is really like from the receptionist than from the company president. I might ask, "How is it to work here?" If I get a frown or a roll of the eyes, that's an important piece of information for me.

I once waited in the lobby of a Los Angeles company for twenty minutes watching an older woman handle a busy switchboard. Several things about the way she did it were striking. First, she spent much of her time standing up, swaying from side to side as she fielded the calls. Second, she seemed to know all the four-digit extensions from memory, though the company had several hundred employees. Third, she ended every brief exchange with a pleasantry. She had a whole library of such phrases. Sometimes it was "Have a very pleasant day, sir," or "I'll be happy to connect you now." I felt as though I was the audience at a one-woman theater performance.

"Do you really have all those extension numbers memorized?" I asked her when there was a momentary lull.

"Honey," she said, "I've been doing this job for ten years. I know everything."

"I'll bet you do," I said, and then, remembering that I was in Los Angeles, added, "If there were an Oscar award for Best Receptionist, you'd get it."

The flattery didn't faze her at all. "You're right!" she replied. And then she lifted her forefinger to signal that the next call was on its way, and our brief conversation ended.

I hoped for her sake she was being well paid. A person like that could give master classes in how to make a boring job interesting.

Once, on my way to Kennedy Airport in New York, my taxi driver was a burly, middle-aged African American man. Within the first five minutes, he had enlightened me with the following facts:

- He had once tried out as defensive end for the Green Bay Packers.

- San Diego had the highest population of heart surgeons per capita of any large U.S. city, a fact he gleaned from the Internet.

- Dr. Charles Drew, the man who developed the procedure for extracting blood plasma, was one of many African American inventors whose contributions were little known or recognized.

In the course of that forty-minute ride, I learned a lot about the reality of working life in America. He wasn't just a cab driver. He had made himself into an educator, a Taxi Professor. When I left his cab, I thanked him for the things he had taught me. He looked me in the eye and nodded, not smiling, but acknowledging my praise. He was serious about his work.

If we think to ourselves "My job is boring. I'm not paid a lot, so I'm not going to contribute a lot. My real vocation is elsewhere," then we have allowed the value and range of our work to be defined by our employer and our paycheck. However, if we are like the Existential Toll-taker, the World's Greatest Receptionist, or the Taxi Professor, then our job can be whatever our creativity can make it.

PRACTICES FOR BOREDOM

- On your way to and from work, listen to all the sounds around you without judgment.

- At least once each day, see if you can listen to others without judgment while you are on the job.

- When you drive, try following a slow driver.

- Once this week, experiment with humor, creativity, and compassion on your job.

N one of us wants to fail. And yet in the course of life failure is inevitable. This is especially true in the workplace, where competition creates both winners and losers. Failure is difficult, but sometimes it can also be an advantage and a sign of strength, particularly for managers or business owners. When a company I once worked for was searching for a new president, all the senior managers received a confidential report from the search firm we had hired. For one candidate, under

the section entitled "Weaknesses," there was a notation that said, "Candidate has not failed."

The search firm considered it a weakness that the candidate had not had an experience of failure. And for good reason. Our company was in trouble. We needed to have somebody who had gone down with the ship, so that if we too started to go down, he or she wouldn't panic and would know what to do.

There is no curriculum to learn how to fail. It is not taught as a subject in business schools, nor can we get credit for it in college. Yet it is one of the most valuable of life experiences, in both a practical and a spiritual sense. And even when we think we are failing, it is hard to know, in the midst of the situation, what is failure and what is not.

Failure is not failure.
Success is not success.
Today is not tomorrow.
You are still you.

FAILURE IS NOT FAILURE

To say "failure" is to make a judgment and a comparison. We put a label on our situation, fixing it in space and time, and measure it against some standard we have set up for ourselves called success. This is not to say that failure is not real. It is. But its reality is tentative and relative. Many times we set ourselves up to fail by the limited or unrealistic way we define success.

I once read a Native American story that illustrated this. The chief of the tribe was proud of his teenage son, who was just of the age to ride with the adult men on one of their periodic raids. The night before the raid, the son fell off his horse and broke his leg. The chief complained bitterly to the tribe's medicine man about this turn of events. "Bad luck," the medicine man agreed.

The raid did not go as planned. The party was ambushed and several of the participants were killed. Many who made it back were wounded or injured. As the chief and the medicine man made the rounds of the survivors, congratulating them on their bravery and comforting the wounded, the chief mentioned to the medicine man that if it weren't for the broken leg, his son might have been killed in the raid along with the others. "Good luck," the medicine man replied.

The medicine man appeared to be agreeing with the chief, but really he was making a point about comparison and judgment. From the chief's point of view at that moment, given what he had already defined as success, the son's broken leg looked like a failure. But the next day, it looked like success.

This kind of ambiguity happens frequently in business. Once, in the early days of my software business, I was upset when a prospective client decided not to purchase our product. I really needed that sale, and not to have it felt like failure to me. My partner pointed out that the client's company seemed shaky, but that observation didn't do anything to fill our skimpy bank account. But my partner was right. Not too many months later, the prospect's company went out of business. If we had taken them on as a client, we would have put in a lot of work and wouldn't have been paid for it. The way it turned out was better for us.

Before I started my own business, I was a consultant to other catalog companies. One such company, a small start-up selling herbal remedies by mail, was struggling. Jonah, the founder, was deeply committed to his products, many of which he produced himself. Jonah was hoping for a big success in the catalog business. A friend of his had started his own catalog business and done extremely well. However, when I examined Jonah's sales figures and response rates, it was clear to me that his business was not going to work as a catalog. As gently as possible, I explained this to him. He listened to my advice, but six months later, I was still receiving his catalog in the mail. As I went on to found my own business, I lost track of Jonah, but recently I saw him featured in the local newspaper. His business was now a chain of small retail outlets and in that form was thriving. In the newspaper article he was candid about his aborted catalog business. "We nearly went under as a catalog," he was quoted as saying, "but in the process we also learned what our customers really wanted, and how to make our business a success."

One of Suzuki Roshi's favorite comments was "Maybe so." He would use it to answer all manner of questions. If a student asked him, "Suzuki Roshi, do you think the Vietnam War is wrong?" he replied, "Maybe so." If we asked, "Is meditation the quickest way to get enlightened?" he gave the same answer.

A student who was enthusiastic about the macrobiotic diet kept pressing Suzuki Roshi to agree that it was the most spiritually advantageous of all diets. Suzuki Roshi didn't really reply to any of these questions, except perhaps to mutter "Maybe so." Finally, after being pestered one last time, he said, "Food is very important."

It might sound as though Suzuki Roshi were just being coy or noncommittal, and at the time it often seemed that way. But now I think he was just being accurate.

If you say to me, "The law office where I work is closing. My last paycheck will be six weeks from now and then I will be on the street. Isn't that terrible?" I might be inclined to echo my teacher and answer, "Maybe so." Not because I am unsympathetic to your plight. It certainly sounds unfortunate. But who knows what will happen? Maybe two years from now you will look back and realize that losing your job was the best thing that ever happened to you.

That is why I say:

Failure is not failure.

Success is not success.

Today is not tomorrow.

You are still you.

What is more important and more essential: that you seem to have failed or that you are still you?

UPLIFT ANOTHER, UPLIFT YOURSELF

"The best way to uplift ourselves is to uplift another" may be a platitude, but it is true, and it is the basis of self-help and self-healing organizations such as Alcoholics Anonymous. If we feel down, everywhere we look is down. If we can create "up" anywhere in our surroundings, whether in ourselves or in someone else, we benefit.

Of course, sometimes that's easier said than done. If our work situation has stagnated, if it has ceased to be a challenge, if it bores and fails to excite us, the last thing we have the energy to do is to encourage someone else. It is more likely that our discouragement will rub off on others, making them feel drained of energy when they are around us.

There are any number of reasons why our work may fail to inspire us. For example, it may not be the work we really wanted to do. When I was in the hospital for an operation, a male nurse took care of me. He was gentle and attentive but seemed a bit sad too. As we got to know each other, he told me that it was his lifelong dream to be a doctor, but his grades were not good enough for him to get into medical school. Being a nurse was the next best thing, and he was quite good at it, but it was not what he really wanted to do. He lived with that regret.

Another possibility is that we are in the classic I'm-a-waiter-but-really-I'm-an-actor situation. Or we worked for years to get a coveted promotion, and it was given to someone else, and now we are locked out of any career advancement. Or, as happened to a great many middle managers and industrial craftspeople in the early 1990s, we were laid off from a secure high-paying job and have had to take a job elsewhere that pays less.

The ultimate solution to many of these situations is a different job, even a different career. But that choice has serious risks and problems of its own. Not everyone can do that. It would be good if the world of employment was not so unforgiving toward people who, through no fault of their own, face reduced circumstances. But that is not the competitive, sometimes heartless, world of work in which we live.

So how can we uplift ourselves in these situations? In a world dominated by money, it runs counter to common sense that we get something by giving something away. But in the world of the spirit, money is not the currency that counts. It has no value there.

Joyce was someone who had one of those waiter-actor jobs. While she studied for her master's degree in psychotherapy, she made her living as a limousine driver. One evening, after dropping off a newlywed couple, she was driving her company's Rolls-Royce by herself, when she was accosted at an intersection by a haggard woman begging from the passing cars. The woman's eyes widened as she saw the Rolls-Royce pull up next to her.

"I don't have any money to give you," said Joyce to the woman. "I only have enough for the bridge toll. But I thought I'd stop anyway, just to say hello."

The panhandler's face softened. "God bless you," she said to Joyce. She patted the shiny black door of the Rolls-Royce. "Look at this Rolls. I'm going to remember this for a long time." She winked at Joyce. "You could give me the car, you know."

Joyce laughed. "If you're here tomorrow, I'll have some money for you."

She made a point of driving by the same corner the next day, but the woman wasn't there.

Someone else at the workshop asked Joyce why she had stopped the car if she knew she didn't have any money. Joyce had to think about that for a while. "I don't know," she said. "My job is pretty boring. I just found myself doing it."

I think she instinctively understood that by reaching out to the woman on the street corner, she was uplifting both of them.

MAKING AN ENERGY SHRINE AT WORK

If things are not going well at work, if we have not been successful, if we are not honored or respected, then what can we do? Should we quit? Perhaps. If you think quitting is a serious possibility, be sure to take a look at the chapter entitled "Quitting." But suppose we can't quit? Suppose, in spite of everything, we don't want to? What can we do?

That depends on our state of mind. If we are agitated, angry, or upset, we need to transform that energy into something more positive, perhaps using some of the practices described in part 2, "Conflict." But suppose we are just discouraged or depressed. Then what?

We don't necessarily need to calm down, to quiet ourselves, to reduce our stress. What we need is something close to the opposite—to get moving, to take action, to raise our energy level so that we have something to work with.

Do you have a picture of your family, or your partner, or your friends on your desk or pinned to the wall at work? You probably do, since this is the most common method of personalizing a work space.

Now let me ask you this: Do you have a picture of your work space or your workmates on your bedside table?

I didn't think so.

Your work life and your personal life are not equivalent. One is clearly more valuable than the other, which is why we decorate our work space with mementos of our friends and loved ones.

Why do we do that? Most people probably don't think about it that much—it is just something that we all do. But if I ask you to think more carefully, you would probably reply that having those pictures at work uplifts you and gives you energy and a sense of purpose. Those pictures, or seashells, or stones, or cartoons, or whatever it is we have collected to personalize our work space function as a kind of shrine to our inner self. They act as a counterweight to our computer monitor, our in-basket, our toolbox or desk lamp.

When we are feeling low, when we are nursing failure or defeat, a shrine like this can be a resource. How long has it been since you have dusted the family pictures on your desktop or rearranged them? How long since you have added to the display of seashells or plastic dinosaurs? To change the shrine, to move it around, to add to it, to take care of it, is to move ourselves and give our inner life a boost. No matter how disappointing things are at work, the shrine represents the part of us that the workplace cannot touch.

Here are some practical suggestions for energizing your workplace shrine.

Add a vase of fresh flowers or a live plant. Besides adding beauty to your work space, a plant requires care—water, food, pruning—or it will die. The plant is you. Like you, the plant is fragile. Like you, the plant needs to be cared for. So care for it regularly, without fail, and you will be caring for yourself. You don't need a spiritual master to explain what it means if you let the plant die.

I have a plant in my office. I call it Audrey III. (Audrey II was the man-eating plant in the musical comedy *The Little Shop of Horrors*.) My plant grows all over the place. It covers my books, sticks in the file cabinet, and gets in the way when I try to close the window. But I don't trim it back. I just water it, and fertilize it, and let it grow. It's the one part of my business that I don't try to manage. I let it manage me. In the movie, Audrey II, the man-eating plant, could talk and would call out to its owner, "Seymour! Feed me!" I sometimes think I can hear Audrey III whispering the same thing.

If you don't work at a desk—if you are a carpenter, for example—try setting up the shrine in your car or truck. If you have one of those models with the cup holders in the armrest, that is a perfect spot for a small potted plant.

Since this is a chapter about failure, add something to the shrine that represents success to you. Perhaps it is a high school medal, or a photo of your wedding day. Maybe it is a rock that you found on a walk during a meditation retreat. Make accomplishment tangible. Turn it into something you can touch and feel.

At least once a week, change something in the shrine. If you ignore the shrine, you are ignoring yourself. If you alter it, you are encouraging inner change and fostering inner resolve. If you don't believe me, neglect the shrine for a few days and then pay attention to it again. See if you can sense the difference.

Keep it private. The shrine needn't look to anyone else like a shrine. In particular, it needn't look religious. You don't need Buddha statues or pictures of masters or saints for the shrine to work. Nor are such things really appropriate for the workplace, which is, after all, not private space. Keep those explicit spiritual images within your own mind, and let them be represented by more neutral objects that symbolize them for you. Don't talk casually about the Energy Shrine to others. To reveal the secret of the shrine lets the positive energy it represents for you leak out.

The workplace shrine represents the swamp, the marshland, and the womb we spoke of earlier, the place where our wounds can heal and new life can spring up. If it seems at first blush to be too simple or obvious, consider that most spiritual practices are just that way—simple and obvious. That is why we tend to walk right by them for the whole of our life. When Suzuki Roshi first taught me meditation, it took him all of fifteen minutes, and I remember thinking "That's it? That's all? He must think I'm a hopeless American too dumb to receive the real stuff." It took me many years—in fact, until I was a teacher myself, giving the same fifteen minutes of instruction to others—to realize fully that the exterior form of real spiritual practice can indeed be quite simple. The secret that makes it work is recognizing that the "real stuff" is you yourself. And you are not simple or obvious.

That's the secret. That's the catch. And that's the fun.

In the movie *Marathon Man,* Dustin Hoffman plays a character who needs to get into his apartment, which is surrounded by armed men waiting to kill him. He goes for help to the neighborhood gang leader, to whom he offers everything of value in the apartment if the gang will break into it for him and retrieve his shoes and gun.

The gang leader is no dope. He says, suspiciously, "What's the catch?"

The Dustin Hoffman character replies, "The catch is it's dangerous."

Slowly a wide grin spreads across the gang leader's face. "That's not the catch. That's the fun."

If you can capture that kind of spirit in your efforts to address Failure, you will not remain despondent for long!

If you are curious to know whom we hired at my former company to be our new president, we brought in someone who had had experience at failing. It was a good thing too, because a year later, in spite of all our efforts, the company nearly went under and had to be sold. Most of the employees, including me, lost their jobs. But our new president managed the whole process quite well. We had the benefit of his strong, steady leadership throughout the crisis. And as a consolation, each of us could go back out into the workplace with that invisible gold star on our résumé, the one that says "Has failed!"

Because of that "failure," I received some severance pay and was forced to think of alternatives to my lost job, which led me directly to start my own business. If I had stayed in my job, my own business would never have happened. Which was the failure? Which was the success?

PRACTICES FOR FAILURE

- Set up a workplace shrine. At least once a week water your plant, touch your objects, move things around.

- Once this week, encourage someone else. Can you feel the effect on yourself?

- The next time you think you have failed, ask yourself, "What is failure? What is success?" How do you define the difference to yourself?

D iscouragement is a general life problem, but it is particularly common at work. Often we find ourselves stuck in a bad situation that we didn't cause and can't escape. Perhaps our boss is unreasonable or uncaring. Perhaps the company is losing ground to a more powerful competitor. Perhaps we have just lost a coveted promotion to a less talented but more aggressive coworker. Perhaps we have some bad habit, like impatience or a quick temper, that keeps getting us into trouble.

When we are discouraged, we want to

give up. We feel that our efforts to change a situation, or to change ourselves, are futile. The fight has gone out of us, and we just want to put our head down and cry.

Strangely enough, from a spiritual standpoint, discouragement can be a real opportunity. When we are discouraged, our ordinary resources for coping are at a standstill. But are our ordinary resources all we have? Or is there something deeper that we can call upon for help? Is there a part of ourselves that cannot be defeated?

Spiritual intention requires a sustained effort to maintain our direction without expecting any result.

ORDINARY INTENTION AND SPIRITUAL INTENTION

"The road to Hell is paved with good intentions." Or so the saying goes. We make a New

Year's resolution to lose weight, we work hard at it for a few weeks, and then our effort lapses and we are reduced to joking about it with our friends. Or we tell ourselves this is the year we are going to learn Spanish. We buy some instruction tapes, and after a few weeks, the tapes just gather dust in our car's glove compartment.

These are examples of ordinary intention, whose success or failure is measured by whether we meet our goal or not. But there is another kind of intention where attaining a goal is secondary, and discouragement is less likely. Spiritual intention is concerned not with short-term success but with the long-term direction of our life. Whether we attain our goal is not as important as our firm commitment to stay pointed in the right direction. It is like a sailor who points the boat at a tree on the distant shore. The boat may sail this way and that. The tree may even disappear from time to time. But the sailor returns again and again to the sight of that tall tree on the horizon. Because we have confidence in that tall tree—our long-term spiritual goal—we are not discouraged, even if our boat seems to be going in circles!

One of the problems of focusing on spiritual as opposed to ordinary intentions is that spiritual intentions are so deeply embedded that it is hard to articulate them or even know what they are. For example, we could say that one of our deepest intentions is to love and be loved, but it would be a little odd to rise up out of bed every morning and say to ourselves, "Today I will try harder to love and be loved!" And it's hardly the sort of sentiment we would want to share with our boss during the annual goal-setting meeting!

Nevertheless, there are more tangible expressions of that deepest intention that we *can* articulate and express. For example, patience, kindness, generosity, cheerfulness, attentiveness, and compassion are all expressions of what a Buddhist would call our Buddha nature—our loving, caring heart. We can pick any one of these to work with and focus on, and make it the treetop on the distant shore at which we point our boat. The phrase "I will try to be more patient today" or just "Patience!" can be our watchword, our breath-by-breath reminder, our silent mantra to repeat at various times during the day. Because such an intention is so deeply rooted, it has much more power than the desire to lose weight or learn Spanish. It draws on the deepest and most nourishing cisterns of our inner life.

And the best way to sustain such a spiritual intention is to keep pointing our boat at the distant tree without any expectation that we will ever get there, letting our intention itself be the goal.

EXPECTING NO RESULT

It may seem odd to speak of making an effort without expecting any result. Isn't that what an intention is, a goal?

We spend our whole childhood and early adulthood learning about goals. That is what school and college train us to do. Get a high grade on the test. Win the game. Set a goal and achieve it. The workplace is no different. We are rewarded for meeting goals and penalized for missing them. Whole departments, divisions, and companies organize their activity around common, well-defined goals. It's hard to imagine a workplace without goals.

But not every aspect of our life is organized around goals.

Think of someone you love—your spouse, partner, or children, for example. Is there a goal in your love? Do you keep score, do you measure whether your love rises to a certain standard? Do you say to yourself, "I'm proud of myself. I love my children twenty percent more than last year. I'm making real progress!"

Of course you don't think that way. The love of your spouse or children is unconditional. It doesn't lend itself to measurement. It is simply a deep, authentic part of who you are.

That kind of love is a good example of a spiritual intention.

The task of raising a child is a nonstop effort, day after day, year after year, for eighteen or twenty years. No one thing we say or do to our child will make that much difference. We will make many mistakes. There will be many setbacks. Yet we never say to ourselves (or almost never), "I'm not going to bother reminding my child not to eat his spaghetti with his hands. He never listens. Besides, no one thing I say is going to make any difference." We don't say that because we love our child and want the best for him, so we continue the effort, regardless of whether he seems to listen.

And at the end of the time, when our child is grown and we can look into his eyes as an adult, what our child has become includes the sum total of everything we said and did while bringing him up.

Is our own life any different? Is the effort we make to continue developing ourselves, for the whole of our life, no matter what our age, any different from the effort to raise a child?

One exercise you might try at work is to make a list on one side of a piece of paper of all the goals you have at work: learn how to make a Web site, increase productivity of your group by 20 percent, achieve vice president by the time you are thirty-five, sign up five thousand new members by June. Then, on the other side of the paper, see if you can describe the part of your work life that is outside the list of goals, the workplace equivalent of your love for your spouse or children. What might that be? Maybe you can't put it into words, maybe it is just a picture, just a circle with sun rays radiating out from it. But perhaps you can feel it. Perhaps you sense that there is some reason why you show up for work every morning that isn't related to conventional achievement.

That ineffable something is spiritual intention. It permeates all of our life, sometimes more visibly than at other times, but it is always there. And because it is always there, it is beyond discouragement, beyond despair. In that wider sense, wherever we point our boat, the tall tree on the distant horizon is there, guiding and encouraging us. Making that effort to turn our boat, over and over again, back to that tall tree is spiritual intention in action.

BIG EFFORT, LITTLE EFFORT

People who practice meditation regularly often find that spiritual practice in the workplace is discouraging because capturing a moment here or there doesn't seem to have any visible or lasting effect. During an extended period of meditation in quiet surroundings, we can actually feel our mind becoming calm, our senses being awakened, our whole body feeling relaxed and light. To many people, that kind of experience is the essence of spiritual practice. But have you ever gone to a gym and tried lifting first light weights and then heavy weights? The light weights are easy. You can lift them many times without tiring. But to lift the heavy weights even once takes tremendous effort.

Doing spiritual practice in the midst of busy activity is like lifting the heavy weights. Just because you can do it only once, for a moment, does not mean that it has no effect. On the contrary, it exercises your spiritual "muscles" as much as doing many repetitions with the light weights, just in a different way.

Traditional meditation is one kind of practice. Capturing moments of self-awareness or self-inquiry during the busy workday is another kind of practice. One cannot be measured against the other. They are each valuable and effective in their own ways. Harry Roberts, who lived for a time down the road from our Buddhist retreat center and often advised us in our farming and gardening work, used to say, "Unless you can take your spiritual practice out of the meditation hall and into your work, it isn't worth a hill of beans." The actual phrase he used was a bit saltier than that, but you get the idea! I can recall Suzuki Roshi saying something similar on many occasions. The two men never knew each other, but I have no doubt they would have gotten along quite well.

REPETITION

When I first began my Buddhist practice in the 1960s, I was like many people of that time in imagining that meditation would lead me to one great spiritual experience that would transform my life. Over time, I learned that while big experiences like that sometimes do occur, the real transformation, the one that really matters, happens moment by moment, day by day. In other words, it is based on patience, confidence, and repetition. It is relatively easy to sustain an effort when you have some clear goal in mind, such as stronger arms or a more attractive body. But when you are discouraged or bored at work, what is going to motivate you to push against your discouragement and find a way through it? To keep coming back to your intention, over and over again, even when it seems you are making no progress at all, is how spiritual practice actually begins to accumulate some staying power. The intention itself becomes the goal. Or to put it another way, we find, over time, that the repetition of our spiritual effort brings us some pleasure.

Lana was an elementary school teacher. She loved working with children but found that their lack of discipline often made her impatient, even angry. Intellectually she knew that they were just children, but emotionally she could not help herself. It bothered her that she could not control her feelings. At some point it became imperative for her to do something about it, so every morning, as soon as she entered the classroom, she said a little prayer to herself: "Today I will not be impatient. Today I will be calm."

Sometime during each day she failed. When I met her, she had already been practicing this way for over two years, and she was becoming discouraged. She didn't feel she was making any progress.

"And how does it feel to do that prayer every morning?"

"The prayer feels good!" she immediately replied. "It's what happens in the rest of the day that is so discouraging."

"I think the prayer is working," I said. "Please keep it up."

"How can the prayer be working?" she objected. "I can't see any improvement."

"You've kept it up for over two years. And it feels good when you do it. That's enough," I replied.

Without quite realizing it, Lana had discovered the pleasure of spiritual repetition, and that pleasure sustained her. To do something over and over again, not for what it can do for you but for its own sake, is real spiritual practice. Lana had it. Her practice was working. I think she was being too hard on herself. Her impatient reactions were slowly, imperceptibly being transformed.

I asked her to be honest and think about the last two years. "Are you sure there has been no improvement?"

She thought about it for a while. "There's been some," she said finally.

"But not as much as you would like."

"No," she admitted, grinning ruefully.

"That's good," I thought to myself. "I know that feeling. If she ever feels satisfied with her improvement, she will stop making the effort."

That kind of effort is something we can all do for the whole of our lives.

Cultivating spiritual intention is like sending a message down a deep well. We can't tell if the message was received. But at the bottom of the well is a splash which signals that the message has arrived. That splash, that ripple in the pond of our habitual patterns of reaction and behavior, is the energy that keeps the intention going.

Can you begin your day with a short phrase, as Lana did, and keep it up even if you see no apparent improvement? How long would you be willing to keep up that kind of effort? For a week, a month, a year?

How about forever?

FINDING YOUR OWN PATH

Spiritual intention stirs things up, not just in ourselves but in the whole situation. Sometimes our effort to practice intention gets a boost from the outer world. Sometimes the message we send down the well sends back an echo.

Katherine worked as a manager in a high-tech firm. Alice managed the department across the hall, and for some reason they clashed from the day they first met. It seemed to Katherine that whatever she tried to do, Alice tried to undermine her. It was never overt, just a feeling.

Katherine decided to try an experiment. One day, as she passed Alice in the hall, she said, "That dress really looks great on you. Where did you get it?" Alice glanced up furtively, muttered, "Saks," and walked quickly away. Not a bad beginning. Every so often, Katherine continued to compliment Alice on some aspect of her style or appearance. Alice's responses, however, were much the same.

Katherine became discouraged. Her intention, valid though it was, wasn't making much of a splash. No message was coming back.

One day, by chance, Katherine ran into Alice in the parking lot. By coincidence, they had parked only one car apart. Katherine was in her vintage Volvo sports sedan and Alice in her BMW. Katherine waved to Alice and caught her eye.

Alice hesitated for a moment and then waved back, with a hint of a smile on her face.

It was a tiny thing, Katherine told the members of our workshop, but it served as a confirmation of her effort. From then on, things were a bit better with Alice. Katherine's modest effort had made enough of a splash over time to be noticed. The message she sent down to the bottom of the well was answered. And her willingness to experiment, to try something new, paid off.

People often imagine that for a spiritual practice to be authentic, it has to be "official," sanctioned by some established spiritual tradition and taught by a qualified teacher. There is some truth to this. But the deepest spiritual practice, the most authentic expression of your spiritual intention, is one that you create yourself.

Suzuki Roshi told us that when he was a novice, his teacher never told him what to do. Sometimes they would go to a parishioner's house to perform a ceremony, such as a memorial service. The young Suzuki was expected to ring the bells and chant the scriptures, but because he hadn't received any instruction, all he could do was fumble about and watch for some clue from his teacher. Then when they got back to the temple, his teacher would scold him for his mistakes! "That's why," Suzuki Roshi explained to us, "when I came to America for the first time I didn't worry about anything. I didn't understand the language very well and the country was new and strange, but I felt fine." He had plenty of experience in finding his own way.

The spiritual path is not like the interstate, with friendly green signs to tell us which exit is which and how to get to Los Angeles or Houston. It is much more like being dropped into the wilderness.

We have to figure out which way to go by moving along, by being curious, by experimenting. Most of all, we need to trust our instincts and our innate sense of direction.

To follow the path, or the Tao, in the ancient Buddhist or Taoist sense, is to explore the terrain of our mind and feelings and to remain open to what we see and hear. The path is not just something we follow, it is something we create as we go. How we make our way through the woods may not be the same as someone else's way. When our friend goes north, we may go south. In this sense, intention functions as our compass. It gives us direction and consistency and allows us to ask ourselves: "Am I following my intention, or have I lost it somewhere along the way?"

CONFIDENCE

To sustain spiritual intention we need an unusual kind of confidence. Instead of being self-assured, in command and in control, we need to develop the ability to feel doubt, to be unsure, to be afraid, and still go forward. This is more than self-confidence. It is confidence in others, in the world, in destiny, in our guardian angel, in God. It is a sense of "it's all right, something will turn up." At the same time, this confidence needs to be more than just wishful thinking. Spiritual confidence is not just a ground cover decorating the surface with pretty flowers. It is more like an unremarkable tree stump with a few green shoots sprouting up out of it and a deep, invisible taproot. By relying on that taproot, any discouragement we feel will quickly dissipate and be replaced by a more fundamental confidence. Discouragement means, literally, a loss of courage. That taproot renews our courage.

Entrepreneurs characteristically have a lot of confidence, but it is not always well rooted. It's my observation that what distinguishes successful entrepreneurs from unsuccessful ones is this difference between deep and shallow roots. I once met a young man who had started a local chain of specialty T-shirt stores while he was in college. Still in his twenties, he whispered to me conspiratorially over a drink that he intended to have his own Lear jet by the time he was thirty. I didn't say anything. In fact, a few years later, his store chain was in bankruptcy and he had been forced out. His confidence was unrealistic, unrooted.

In contrast, my good friend Mitchell, having lost his job as a financial services executive, had hung out his shingle as a personal financial consultant. "How is it going?" I asked him a few months after he began.

"Not many clients," he said. "Living off credit cards."

"Worried?" I asked sympathetically.

He just made his eyes big and nodded. But there was something cheery about his worry—a grounded, good-hearted feeling. Mitchell was a person you could trust. I trusted him, and a year later, the many new clients who had eventually flocked to him confirmed that others could too. His confidence included some uncertainty, some fear and doubt, as well it should have, given the risks he was taking. But eventually, his attitude paid off.

What makes this kind of confidence really work is the principle of interconnection. Interconnection means that everything in the world is connected to everything else. It also means that the effect of our thoughts, feelings, and actions doesn't disappear. It continues to radiate outward, like a ripple in a pond. For example, if we form a strong intention to be more kind to our coworkers, even once, the effect of that resolve will continue to operate beneath the surface for a long time afterward, even if we think we are making no progress in realizing it.

We have been taught to trust the evidence of our senses, to accept as real what we can see and hear, touch and smell. That is our scientific bias. But there is another kind of reality, more subtle and less evident on the surface of the world, that has to do with the connections between things.

If we judge the effect of our intention only on the visible result, we will quickly become discouraged and give it up. But if, like a gardener pouring water into sand, we have confidence that the effect of our effort will sink down into the roots of our situation and provide nourishment where we cannot see it, then we will be able to persevere.

There are many Buddhist stories about the power of a single thought. One story concerns a rabbit that is pursued by a starving tiger. As the tiger closes in and the rabbit cowers in fear of his life, the rabbit thinks, "I feel compassion for this starving tiger because I know how it feels to be hungry. I will allow myself to be eaten, so that in a future life I may be born as a human being and attain enlightenment."

Such folktales are teaching stories to illustrate the staying power of a pure thought, of spiritual intention. They are based on a worldview that understands a thought to be as real as a house.

We all know the saying "It's all in your mind!" which generally means "It isn't real!" Einstein's formula $E = mc^2$ was all in his mind, too, at the time he discovered it. A few years later, a bomb exploded over Hiroshima and changed the world. Which was more real, Einstein's thought or the bomb that his thought helped create? Which is more real, our intention or the actions that flow from our intention?

A Buddhist would say that, if anything, the thought is more real, because it is the source of the action. So we must pay attention to our thoughts, and our feelings, and the whole of our inner life. It is the source of how we choose to act and to live.

MAKING YOUR OWN LUCK

Developing this kind of confidence depends on paying close attention to what is going on around us. We all know people who seem to have all the luck. However, luck can often be a knack for noticing seemingly insignificant events in the background of a situation and taking that as a cue to act.

Justin was an entrepreneur who had invented his own product—a measuring instrument for structural engineers—and had formed a company to bring it to market. The engineering community wasn't aware that such an instrument existed. In fact, they had gotten by for their whole careers without it. For Justin's company to be successful, he would need to educate those engineers before he could sell to them.

Justin had all the usual pressures and problems of a start-up—cash flow, meeting payroll, and competition, not to mention long hours. After three years, his seed money was nearly gone, two of his key employees were deferring half of their salaries every month, and Justin himself was paying his mortgage with credit cards. It looked as though he wasn't going to make it.

One day, after yet one more frustrating sales presentation—the engineers in his audience liked his product but said they didn't see any immediate application for their businesses—Justin noticed that one of the engineers had picked up his product and was examining it closely in his hands, his eyes only a few inches from the calibration meter. Justin went over to the man to retrieve his sample and go home.

"Nice," the engineer said, as he handed the instrument back to Justin.

Something about the way that engineer said "nice" gave Justin an extra boost. His battered confidence returned. He decided to take out one more loan and give the company three more months. Within those three months, his first big order came in. A year later, his staff had doubled and his business was on its way to turning its first profit.

Sometimes one word is enough to change our luck, if we are attentive enough to hear it.

PRACTICES FOR DISCOURAGEMENT

- Verbalize a spiritual intention, such as "I will try to be more patient." Even saying the single word "Patience" will do.

- Make your intention focused and specific. If "Patience" is too broad, try "Patience on the telephone."

- At least twice a day, verbalize the intention to yourself—once as you are entering your workplace and once as you are leaving.

- When you find yourself forgetting your intention, say to yourself "Forgot!" and then repeat your intention.

- Don't look for any result. If you find yourself thinking "This isn't doing any good!" set that thought aside. Repeat your intention.

part four

INSPIRATION

THE SECTOR of Inspiration includes such states as creativity, ambition, excitement, and joy. Inspiration states are high energy, but unlike Conflict states, we enjoy them. When we are fully absorbed and engaged in our work, we have energy to spare. We can give freely of ourselves and feel not lessened but magnified. As Harry Roberts said in chapter 1, "To find joy in your work is the greatest thing for a human being."

The author Aldous Huxley once remarked to an interviewer, "All my life I have been paid well to write, which I love and would have done for nothing!" If you have this experience with your paying job, then good for you! You are one of the lucky ones. More commonly, if people have this experience at all, they have it not with their day jobs but with their hobbies or avocations. Wander through your neighborhood on a sunny weekend and stop to chat with your neighbor at work in her rose garden or with her husband hunched over a wood carving in the garage. Listen to them as they describe their activities, for which they are being paid nothing, and see the glow in their faces, the care and attention in their movements. Theirs is a wonderful job. They do indeed find joy in their work.

But even if all of us had the job of our dreams, the best job is not always wonderful. High-energy states, whether positive or negative, tend to be unstable, oscillating between inspiration, creativity, and excitement on the one hand and stress, difficulty, and worry on the other. Think of a movie director juggling schedules, or a software developer working toward a due date, or a newspaper reporter struggling to file a major story before the deadline. Every hour, every minute, is a roller-coaster ride.

I know. I have been that software developer working toward that deadline. I have ridden the roller coaster. Remember when we talked about the string of colored popcorn in chapter 3, red for stressful, blue for sad, golden for contented, and green for inspiring? The high-energy realm can feel like green light, red light, green light, red light! That is why the focus of this section is on negotiating those transitions, those peaks and valleys, in a way that develops rather than defeats us.

The Hot Positive energy of Inspiration is balanced somewhat precariously between Conflict and Stagnation. Lean too far to one side, and we plunge back into the unwholesome territory of Hot Negative—anger, worry, and fear. Lean too far to the other, and we slip down into Cool Negative—disappointment, depression, and failure. We have all experienced short periods of Inspiration at work: the schoolteacher who helps her class to put on a pageant, the sales manager who exhorts her team to exceed its goal, or the late nights and weekends preparing for an important presentation! We can easily become swept up in such efforts for as long as they last. But to sustain that kind of effort in the long run requires a more dispassionate kind of energy. There needs to be some part of us that can ask "How is this going? Is this really what I want to do? Is this really satisfying?"

This section will explore four areas where we confront these questions. In the first, we will explore ambition—its positive and negative sides, as well as its potential to contribute to spiritual growth. In the second, we will examine time and money and challenge the conventional wisdom that time *is* money. In the third, we will explore forgiveness—its importance in the workplace and its characteristics as an intense, Hot Positive energy. And in the fourth, we will talk about the most problematical Inspiration of all—quitting!

I once had a friend—let's call him Jason—who was an excellent high school teacher. All of his students' parents said so, and the students loved him. He was innovative, experimental, and creative. Visitors to his classroom were struck by the buzz of energy and curiosity that filled the room.

For many years, Jason felt that he had found his true calling. But eventually he was no longer satisfied being a teacher. Secretly he yearned to be like his sister, who was a

wealthy, successful surgeon. He dreamed of living in a bigger house, of being able to drive a Maserati convertible with the top down. He searched for some alternative occupation that would allow him to earn more money and decided to take a job selling real estate. His prospective employer, a young entrepreneur with a brash manner and a Mercedes sports car, wooed him with visions of the quick wealth that could be made in the hot real estate market.

Jason marched into his principal's office and gave the tell-off-your-boss speech that all of us have fantasized from time to time. He told the principal how unimaginative and dull he was, how unpleasant it was to work for him, how stodgy and bureaucratic the school system was. He gave the speech, experienced

You know what your problem is, Rocco? You want more.

from the movie
Key Largo

a rush of liberation and relief, and then walked out of his school, his job, and his career.

Jason had not chosen wisely. The real estate boom in the Northeast, where he lived, suddenly crashed. There were no riches to be had there. Jason, frustrated and depressed, began living off his teacher's retirement fund. He dabbled in drugs. His family fell apart. His wife filed for divorce.

The saddest part of this story is that Jason was luckier than most. He had found his calling—teaching young adults—and was making a good living doing it. That's more than many people ever do. And yet he threw it over to chase an ill-formed, inappropriate dream. He was a born teacher, a genius in the classroom, and ill suited for the life of a salesman. Even if he had made a killing in real estate, in all likelihood he would not have been happy.

One of the strong points of our capitalist system is that it encourages and rewards ambition. The desire to do better for yourself, your children, and your family, the urge to invent, to innovate, to explore, and to create, can be a positive force for good in the world. But it has its dark side. Ambition is intertwined with greed, with the pursuit of money, status, and power. Ambition can easily become not a means to an end but an end in itself—harmful, addictive, and destructive.

What is the spiritual approach toward ambition? Is there a legitimate place for worldly ambition in spiritual life? How can a spiritual attitude temper ambition and keep it from deteriorating into blind avarice? My friend Jason truly thought he was following the American Dream—reach higher, take chances, go for the gold. Instead, he destroyed everything he cared about. He was neither a bad person nor a foolish one. On the contrary, he was smart, caring, compassionate, and had a sincere spiritual dimension to his life. What went wrong?

You have learned by now that I like to use movies as illustrations, so indulge me one more time as I invoke one of my favorites: *Key Largo,* starring Humphrey Bogart as the cynical war hero with a heart of gold and Edward G. Robinson as Rocco, the gangster. Consider this pithy exchange:

BOGART: You know what your problem is, Rocco? You want *more*.

ROBINSON *(taking the cigar from his mouth with a grin of delight)*: Yeah! That's right. I want *more!*

Now, "more" is not in itself bad. It is legitimate to want more. In fact, the workplace is one of the prime areas in our lives where our search for more can bear fruit. The desire to learn new skills, to serve, to find a better, more fulfilling job, to contribute to making the world a better place, and to leave a lasting legacy are all important and valid goals, in both a material and spiritual sense. But there is a fine line between ambition and greed, risk and foolishness, wanting more and never being satisfied without more. Rocco the gangster wanted more not for any higher purpose but for the pure thrill of it. He wanted more because he did not have a life or a character that recognized the value of what he had, and "more" was all that kept him going. His criminal personality cared little for the consequences of his actions on others, as long as it satisfied that craving for the next thing, for *more*.

There is a bit of Rocco in everyone, I think. Part of what fuels our desire to do better, to have more for ourselves and our family, to reach higher and dream bigger, is that primitive desire for more. When Rocco grins and says, "Yeah! That's right. I want *more!*" he is to some extent speaking for all of us. What is memorable about these lines is that *more* is not an adjective, but a noun. Rocco doesn't just want more security, more recognition, more satisfaction, he wants more of everything, more as an end in itself.

This difference is what distinguishes legitimate ambition from greed. Being able to understand and manage that difference is the subject of this chapter. If my friend Jason, in his restlessness with teaching, had been able to distinguish between his legitimate ambition on one side and his envy and dissatisfaction on the other, he might have been able to catch himself before he fell so far so fast. At the critical moment, the two became confused in his mind and he acted without regard to the possible consequences. Ambition made him blind.

I would like to say that Buddhism has a family of practices ready-made to cope with this issue, but worldly ambition is one of those areas where Buddhism suffers from being an ancient, rather than modern, tradition. Buddhism does recognize that pride is one of the more intractable mental states, even for people of advanced spiritual stature. To judge from the amount of attention paid to it in traditional texts, pride was as much a problem in ancient Buddhist monasteries as ambition is in today's corporate offices. But monastic pride is a far cry from the worldly ambition of the modern workplace.

When I lived in a Buddhist retreat center thirty years ago, we saw the workplace as a distraction from our spiritual practice. It was common for my Buddhist friends, many of whom had graduate degrees, to take a job that made few demands and allowed them to concentrate on spiritual study.

I am grateful for my years of monklike simplicity. They made me understand, in a way no book ever could, how much of what we think we need is not really necessary. Consumer economies run on the principle that the more people want, the better. If our desires begin to fatigue, if we begin to think that we have enough, advertisers will bombard us with television ads, billboards, telemarketing calls—anything they can do to change our minds and start us wanting more again.

Suzuki Roshi used to say that there was only one legitimate desire, and that was to be spiritually awakened. Indeed, if we focus on the fact that someday we will die and all that we have done in our life will be lost to us, then Suzuki Roshi's attitude makes good sense.

But most of us, not being monks, don't really live that way. We live as though all that we strive for really matters, if not to us, then to our children, our community, and our society. And it does matter. All our efforts to grow, to develop, and to contribute are the essence of human community. We plan ahead, visualize our career moving forward, imagine the heights we ultimately hope to achieve, and look forward to the ease of our retirement.

WHAT DO YOU REALLY WANT?

If we live like a saint, with few desires, then ambition is not an issue for us. But if we don't, then we should at least be honest with ourselves about what our main desires are and why we have them. One reason Jason's ambition defeated him was that he was not really clear about what he wanted. What made his heart sing was working with kids. Anyone who watched him in the classroom could see that, and if he had been scrupulously honest with himself, he would have been able to see it too.

From one point of view, Suzuki Roshi was right. The deepest desire we all share is to comprehend what Buddhists call "the great matter of life and death." But even Suzuki Roshi would probably admit that that is not our *only* legitimate desire, simply the deepest one. There are many other desires that are not only legitimate but spiritually rewarding. The desire to have a job that is reasonably satisfying, that isn't abusive or exploitative, and that doesn't offend our ethical sense is part of what Buddhism means by "Right Livelihood," which we will be discussing in more detail in chapter 17. Right Livelihood is an important aspect of the Buddhist spiritual path, and it is in pursuit of an appropriate livelihood that ambition serves our spiritual ideals best.

PRACTICING WITH AMBITION

While traditional Buddhism does not have practices that work directly with ambition on the job, there are some that address it indirectly. The two that seem most appropriate for an exploration of ambition are Truthful Feeling and Truthful Effort.

The practice of Truthful Feeling poses a simple question: How do you feel just now? Do you feel good, or bad, or neutral? This is not "feeling" in the sense of love, excitement, or anger, but a more primitive quality of positive or negative, pleasant or unpleasant. We share this faculty with the whole animal kingdom. Watch a dog or a cat as it negotiates its way through the day; in each situation it is making up its mind—I like this, I don't like that.

What is problematical about us human beings is that we have an amazing capacity to fool ourselves about whether something pleases us or not. When we ask ourselves "How do I feel just now about my work? Do I really enjoy this job or not?" what may come to mind are all our conflicting thoughts, opinions, and emotions about the job—it was better than the last job, it pays so well, the commute is short, the people are nice—rather than our basic feeling about the job itself, which, in Buddhist tradition, boils down to one of three answers:

1. I like it.

2. I don't like it.

3. I neither like it nor dislike it, that is, I'm neutral.

This sense of aversion versus attraction lies very deep in our psyche. To like or dislike, to be attracted or repulsed, is basic to all life. That is why it is so important for each of us to be aware of it and connected to it.

Jason is an example of someone who was out of touch with his fundamental likes and dislikes. His head was so full of ideas about the kind of person he would like to be, the kind of car he would like to drive, and the kind of impression he would like to make on his sister's friends that he managed to convince himself that he didn't like teaching, when actually he loved it.

As a counterexample, consider the case of Emily, a school principal beloved by her colleagues, the schoolchildren, and their parents. But she herself found her job increasingly stressful and unrewarding, so much so that she began to see a therapist. After a few months of therapy, she came to realize that in spite of her outward success, school administration was not what she really wanted to do. She quit her job and today is far happier as a self-employed caterer.

The practice of Truthful Effort is not quite as simple. Truthful Effort is about motivation. While Truthful Feeling asks how, Truthful

Effort asks why. The practice of Truthful Effort explores the question "Why am I doing this? What is my purpose?" When we steer a sailboat, if all we are doing is heeling the boat into the wind so that it will go fast, without having a clear destination in mind, we will quickly lose our way. Truthful Effort helps us find a beacon toward which we can steer the boat.

Now let's take a closer look at these two practices.

TRUTHFUL FEELING

A common technique used in psychotherapy is for the therapist to ask "How do you feel about that?"

When we are asked such a simple, straightforward question, in the intimacy of the therapeutic session, sometimes a door opens in our heart and for a moment we can be completely honest with ourselves. In response to the therapist's question, we might find ourselves blurting out, "I feel very angry about it!" And then we are surprised, because we did not realize, until the therapist asked us, that we felt that way.

The spiritual practices of Buddhism predate psychotherapy by two millennia, but some of them resemble the therapeutic dialogue. When we ask ourselves the question "How do I feel?" we are on the same path of self-discovery as the Buddha.

The Buddha himself began life with a serious case of job dissatisfaction. He was born a prince and was in training to be the king. Throughout his teens and his twenties, he enjoyed all the benefits of the royal life—wealth, servants, concubines, power. But little by little a nagging thought kept haunting him: "I don't really like this. This is not satisfying." Eventually the Buddha quit his lucrative job as crown prince and took up another occupation, that of ascetic wanderer. Thus the great wisdom tradition we know as Buddhism began with one man's transformation of ambition.

Practicing Truthful Feeling uses the same technique of Raising the Question that we discussed in chapter 5. With Truthful Feeling, however, the practice is much less free-form. In fact, we only ask one question: "How do I feel about my job just now?" And there are only three possible answers: I like it, I don't like it, or I don't know!

If, when you try the practice, you are tempted to embellish your answer—"Well, I like it most days, but my boss makes me so angry!"—then you are departing from the ground of Truthful Feeling and have been diverted into the labyrinth of thinking and emotion. Keep bringing yourself back to the root question: "How do I feel about my job just now?"

Sometimes it takes a shock for us to know for sure how we really feel. I once had a conversation at a meditation retreat with a middle school teacher named Gail. Gail explained that she taught eighth-grade English to a largely Latino population; many of the boys were at risk from gangs and drugs, and the girls were prone to drop out of school to work for the family. Gail told me that the previous summer she had had a near-death experience. Highly allergic to bee stings, she was stung while hiking in the woods. By the time the paramedics arrived, she had gone into shock and was barely conscious.

"I felt myself leaving my body. I wasn't afraid. I felt quite calm. I could hear the paramedics working on me, but I was somewhere else. It seemed as though I had a choice. I could just keep going and float away, or I could come back. For a while, I wasn't sure which I was going to do. I had had a good life. I was happy with what I had accomplished.

"And then I thought about my kids at school. It's a hard job being their teacher. There are many days I think to myself, 'I'm too old for this.' But then I remember how much difference I can make. They're young enough to listen and pay attention. I know that for some of them my influence was critical in turning them around. I realized that I didn't want to die. I wanted to come back for my kids.

"When I regained consciousness, the paramedics said that they thought they were losing me but that suddenly my blood pressure and vital signs became normal. That's when I opened my eyes. They couldn't explain it but said it was not the first time they had seen it happen." When faced with the ultimate choice, with life or death, Gail had realized how she really felt. She reached a place in herself of naked truth, and that truth carried her back to life.

Max had the opposite experience. When I first knew him, he was a classic workaholic. Ask Max how he felt about his job as a stockbroker and he would invariably say, "It's great! I love it!" All the while his health and family life were suffering.

Max and I were good enough friends for me to know that he was not being honest with himself. I could tell that he didn't like his work at all. He had been trained as a musician, but like many talented artists, he couldn't translate that skill into a viable livelihood. When he would tell me how much he loved his work, how much he thrived on the challenge, the gamesmanship, the hustle and bustle, I could sense that underneath all of that was his pain at not being able to do what he really loved—music.

One evening while we were having dinner at a Mexican restaurant, I decided to confront him directly. "Max, in your heart of hearts, wouldn't you rather go back to playing your violin?"

"What?" he exclaimed bitterly. "And starve to death?"

"I'm not asking you about what it would pay. I'm asking you about what you love."

Max hung his head and stared down at his enchilada. "It's too late for that," he muttered.

Over time, Max and I drifted apart. The last I had heard, he and his wife were getting a divorce.

Like many people, Max had abandoned a less-than-lucrative first love for a livelihood that was stifling him. He told himself that he had been successful in his quest for financial security—and he had—but his true ambition, the one that could have truly fulfilled him, had been sacrificed. We can all sympathize with Max. I certainly did, because when I was twenty I did the same thing. I too walked out on a promising career as a musician and composer. It is very difficult to make a living as a musician or any professional in the arts. I will never pass a saxophonist on the sidewalk or the subway without putting a few dollars in his or her hat. I think I give the money not just to help the musician but in recognition of my own path not taken.

If Max had been able to own up to his actual feeling, if he could have touched his own grief and regret, it might have helped. It might even have steered him into a livelihood that would have left room for membership in a community orchestra or amateur chamber group. He could have volunteered to perform in hospitals or convalescent homes. My mother, a retired music teacher, used to go several times a week to convalescent homes, where she played the piano and sang songs to seemingly catatonic Alzheimer patients. She told me moving stories about how their heads would raise up when they heard the music, how their hands started to wave in time with the beat, and how some of them even managed to sing along, even though they never said a word the rest of the week.

If Max had been able to go all the way into answering the question "How do you feel?" I suspect that he and his wife would still be together, and his life, his work, and his love for music would be more fulfilling.

Max's story illustrates how the modern workplace forces us to make choices that keep us from being fully ourselves. To those who would argue that our hard-working, high-tech culture has granted us unparalleled wealth and a high standard of living, I would answer: Go to any country in the developing world. Go to Bali, or to India, or to China, or to Africa—or for that matter, go to the Amish country of Pennsylvania or Ohio. Travel to the countryside and watch people working together. Look into their faces. Listen to them sing their work songs as they plow their fields or cast their fishing nets. Yes, third-world people are often undernourished, uneducated, or ill. And what most of them want is to be like Americans. And yet when I reflect on the surge of interest in spirituality in America, and the fascination with sacred cultures like that of Tibet, I sense that there is some part of the traditional, preindustrial way of life that we would like to have back.

We must be careful not to romanticize the life of third-world poverty. It is a grim life, difficult and often cut short. But it is sobering to realize that there are many ways in which our modern way of life compares unfavorably with traditional societies. We have gained a lot, but we have also given up a lot.

What is your true feeling about your work? How do feel about your job right now?

Don't be like Jason, whose ambition made him blind. But be

careful of falling into the trap that caught Max, of giving up on your dream and your true satisfaction because it did not come true the way you wanted. Somewhere in the middle of all of that lies your true feeling and your legitimate ambition.

And if the answer to the question "How do you feel about your work?" is that you don't know, or don't feel anything in particular, that is all right. Perhaps that means your job isn't very engaging one way or the other. In that case, the section on Stagnation may have some useful suggestions for you. Or it may mean that you are truly ambivalent—some parts you like and some you don't. That's all right too.

Just keep asking the question and don't be surprised if your inner voice responds with a variety of answers from one day to the next. There is no rule that says we will always feel the same about what we do. It is the process of asking and the long-term outcome of that sustained effort that is important.

TRUTHFUL EFFORT

Truthful Effort is also a questioning practice, but the question it asks is "Why am I doing this job? What is my reason and my purpose?" This kind of questioning needs to go beyond the obvious answers—"To make a living," "To serve others"—to a more penetrating inquiry. Every job supplies you with a paycheck, so why do this particular one? And there are many ways to serve others. Is the one you have chosen really the most satisfying?

Another way of asking the question is to say "What needs are being fulfilled by this job?" If you want to be thorough about this inquiry, it may help to make a list. Be as honest as you can. Do any of the following answers resonate for you?

To add something of value to the world.
To help others.
To make a new scientific discovery.
To rise to the top.
To prove to the world (or my friends, or my parents, or
    myself) that I can do it.

To retire early.
To have time to write poetry.
To be famous.
Everyone in my family is a doctor.
I love to cook.
I love people.

To produce an answer like "To be famous" requires a considerable degree of self-candor. Most people would not admit to such a motivation, but many of us have it. Our celebrity society encourages it. And if that is our answer, the exercise can continue from there: "Why be famous? What is valuable about that?" Truthful Effort is a continuous process of digging deeper and deeper into ourselves until we discover our deepest desire and our true calling.

How do we know when we have found it?

There is no magic answer, but one characteristic about work that is truly satisfying that I have observed in myself and others is that it does not seem like work but play.

In many figures of speech, play is the opposite of work. "All work and no play makes Jack a dull boy." "Work hard, play hard." We call something easy by saying it is "child's play."

Child's play! Anyone who spends much time with children can only marvel at their inexhaustible energy and how diligently they devote themselves to playing their games. Before you try to answer the question of what motivates you to work hard, you might ask: What motivates children to play hard?

No one tells them to do it. Certainly no one pays them to do it. In fact, if someone were to pay them to do it—for example, if you were to walk up to a group of children on a playground and give each of them a five-dollar bill and say, "I want you to play for an hour"— I have no doubt that they would immediately pocket the money. But your request would contaminate their activity. It wouldn't be play anymore.

Both work and play require effort, but there is something different about the energy of play. There is an inbred pleasure to it, a spontaneity, a sense of being one with the activity. Work is more sober, more scripted, more defined. Why do you work? Why do you play? What is the difference?

Do you remember the Existential Toll-taker, who greeted every car with the words "Howdy, big spender!"? That was a kind of play, one that he was able to integrate—or, perhaps, get away with—on his job. When I was checking in for my flight home from New York recently, the ticket agent asked me the usual security questions about my baggage and then added with a wry grin, "And what's your shoe size and blood type?"

"Is that how you manage asking those same questions day after day?"

"You got it, honey," she said. "I'm a New Yorker," she added. "Humor is what gets me through the day."

What is most distinctive about play is that there is no room for dishonesty or self-deception about it. When we can play at our work seriously, the way children do when they are totally devoted to building a sand castle or playing hide-and-seek, a safe haven opens up within us, a kind of freedom. It's not easy to sustain. I can't claim to run my business the way a child builds a sand castle. Much of the time I am immersed in it and totally serious about it.

But not always. There are moments when the feeling changes. Sometimes when I am deep in the throes of computer programming, I find myself fiddling with the program just to make it more elegant, more beautiful. No one but another programmer would ever know the difference, but I know. That feeling is a lot like play. There is a lightness to it, a joy that is entirely different from the feeling of doing a job.

That feeling transforms ambition—in my case, the ambition to be a successful software entrepreneur—into something quite different. Ambition is no longer a goal to be achieved; rather, it brings a quality of joy, even love, that needs no goal. I think that is what Harry Roberts must have meant when he said "To find joy in your work is the greatest thing for a human being."

Jason had joy in his work, he just let lesser ambitions take over. Max knew joy. He just couldn't find a way to sustain it in his current work life. Emily, the school principal who became a caterer, realized that she was not experiencing joy in her work and followed her heart until she did.

That feeling of joy is the Hot Positive aspect of ambition. It is ambition as Inspiration.

"Howdy, big spender!"

"What's your shoe size and blood type?"

What word or phrase might open the garden of play, and the joy of work, for you?

PRACTICES FOR AMBITION

- How do you feel just now? Give your feeling a description: good, bad, or indifferent.

- How do you feel about your work just now: good, bad, or indifferent?

- What is your deepest ambition?

- Are you practicing Truthful Effort now? How can you introduce the spirit of play into your work?

W hat do the world's great religions have to say about the relationship of spirituality to money? Jesus drove the money changers from the temple. Saint Paul said, "The love of money is the root of all evil." In some Buddhist traditions monks are prohibited from touching money. Orthodox Jews cannot spend money on the Sabbath, and in Islam, charging interest for a loan is considered wrong.

The great spiritual traditions all seem to agree: Money and spirituality do not mix. There

is something about money that seems to draw us away from ourselves, that clouds our vision. People will cheat for money, they will lie, steal, even kill—all for something that has little intrinsic value in itself and is ultimately nothing more than an elaborate social agreement. Christianity, Judaism, Buddhism, and Islam all came into being at a time in human history when money was a relatively new invention. Perhaps the founders of these great religions saw with their own eyes how money changes the way people treat each other.

Time is not money.
Time is spirit.
Time is love.

If you ask people why they work, they will usually say, "To make money, to make a living." In fact, work that doesn't earn money usually isn't called work—it's called a hobby or volunteering. Money is what makes a job a job.

Attitudes about money have changed over

the past thirty years. When I graduated from college in 1967, I was like many of my generation in feeling that what was important was not to make money but to live with integrity, to do good in the world, to be emotionally and spiritually fulfilled. Even though I graduated from a prestigious college and could have entered a lucrative profession, I went to a Christian seminary and eventually found my way into a Buddhist monastery. At the time I gave little thought to my financial future.

Those of us who grew up in the fifties and sixties weren't fully aware of how wealthy the United States was compared to the rest of the world. It was easy then for a college graduate to get by without much thought of money. In the nineties, it is different. A recent survey by the American Council on Education showed that 75 percent of today's college freshmen said that their top goal was "to be well off financially" compared with 40 percent in 1970. Only 41 percent today said they wanted to "develop a meaningful philosophy" of life compared with 83 percent in 1967.

When I graduated from college, I was one of those 83 percent and spent the next fifteen years in a Buddhist retreat center. Besides being able to meditate and thoroughly study the Buddhist tradition, I got a taste of how it was to live without much concern for money. It also made my reentry into the workplace, at age thirty-five, rather unusual. I did not come into it with the perspective of a job seeker but with the outlook of a monk. I quickly became successful, in a conventional sense, but the monk that I used to be stood off to the side saying, "I am making a good income, while four years ago, as the head of a retreat center, I made a tenth as much. I'm the same person, with the same skills. What's different?"

What was different, of course, is that in my new job I was doing something that my for-profit employer (and its customers) valued highly in monetary terms. Another difference was that I was experiencing anew the *energy* of money—money as motivating, inspiring, attractive, seductive, powerful—at an age when most people are long accustomed to it.

My spiritual training did not prepare me for this. So I was left to mull over the question "What is money, really, and how does it relate to our spiritual life?"

A MEDITATION OF MONEY

Buddhism includes many different meditations: meditation on the breath, meditation on compassion, even meditation on colored wheels and sacred paintings. It lacks a meditation on money, probably because Buddhist monks were prohibited from handling it, but it does have many meditation practices dealing with greed. While greed is a psychological state, money is physical, palpable, measurable. That is one reason why it is so powerful. It can function as a universal measure of value and be transferred from one person to another. While greed remains within us, money can go anywhere. It seems to have an independent reality, a life of its own.

But does it really? How much do our own mental attitudes, desires, and projections affect, even create, the reality of money? How does money influence our perceptions and actions in the workplace? These are the questions this chapter will explore.

Let us begin our meditation on money by examining the physical object. From your wallet or purse, take out the highest denomination of currency you have. Probably it will be a twenty-dollar bill. That is fine, but a hundred-dollar bill works even better. A hundred dollars is a lot of money. It gets your attention. So let's imagine that we have the hundred-dollar bill before us.

We look at it. Peering back at us is the kindly face of Benjamin Franklin. In each corner are large numerals indicating that this piece of green paper is one hundred times more valuable than a nearly identical one that has only the numeral 1 on it. Of course, a hundred-dollar bill has no more intrinsic value than a one-dollar bill; they both cost the U.S. Treasury exactly the same number of pennies to manufacture. The greater worth of the Ben Franklin picture is determined by social agreement, convention, and law. It is a root agreement, like our understanding that the week shall have seven days, or that the hours of the day shall be twenty-four. These matters were all up for grabs at one time. It is only with the passage of centuries that these originally arbitrary arrangements have come to have the force of law, of inevitability, of reality itself.

Money is one more manufactured reality. We can, with some effort, trace back the history of money to its roots. But having done that, what more can be said? One cannot go into a bank and complain that the crisp new hundred is a fiction, and you would like something of "real" value, say a gold coin. Our right to do that vanished in the 1930s, and asking for silver coins became obsolete in the 1970s. Besides, what makes the gold or silver coin any more "real" than the paper except its weight and shine?

Let's continue our meditation with an experiment. In ancient times, Buddhist monks would stare for long periods of time at a disk of yellow clay, until they could perfectly visualize the object with their eyes closed. So let's try something similar here. Put the bill in front of you, say on the kitchen table, and stare at it for a while.

If I ask you, "What is it?" what would you say?

If you say, "Well, it's a greenish piece of paper with a picture of Ben Franklin on it," I would challenge you by replying, "If that were so, you could drop it on a busy sidewalk and it would stay there for more than a few seconds."

If you say, "It's a hundred-dollar bill. I could buy a week's worth of food with it," I might reply, "No it's not. It's just a green piece of paper. Besides, how do you know it's a real hundred-dollar bill? Maybe it's counterfeit."

In fact, counterfeit technology is so good these days that only experts, with advanced equipment, can identify the best ones.

As a practical matter, what makes a hundred-dollar bill real versus counterfeit is everyone's belief that it is real. When you go to spend the hundred dollars, your belief in its reality and the belief of the department store clerk who accepts it conspire to produce a shopping bag in your hand. It is all a choreographed game in which we are trained from childhood.

When we read that an ordinary hair dryer once owned by

Jacqueline Onassis sold at auction for five thousand dollars, or that a desiccated piece of seventy-year-old cake from the wedding of the Duke of Windsor went for twenty-five thousand dollars, we are reminded that money ultimately represents a thought or idea that may have little to do with real value or worth. Money can represent real needs, like food or shelter, but more often it measures the strength of an abstract desire. Money represents our image of ourselves, our public self. In some way we barely understand, it *is* the self.

Now let's perform another meditation experiment. Next to the hundred-dollar bill, place a one-dollar bill.

Look at the one-dollar bill.

Now look at the hundred-dollar bill.

What changes within you when you shift your gaze from one to the other?

You may not be able to sense it right away, but suppose you were to drop first one, then the other, through a grate in the sidewalk, losing it forever. Do you think your heart would beat the same in both cases, or that you might not curse vigorously in one case?

The greater value you assign to the hundred-dollar bill does not reside in the physical object itself. It is something you have been taught, something you have accepted and internalized because it is fundamental to the social fabric. You give it value because everybody else does. That value is a kind of collective visualization, a made-up creation that has become real because we have all agreed to make it real.

It is difficult to step outside of this framework. When I do this meditation in workshops, at first people are fascinated with the physical object. They are surprised to find that they have used money their whole lives without ever having looked closely at it. They notice that the piece of currency they are holding is among other things a work of art, an artist's engraving with trees, buildings, and abstract designs, not to mention cryptic notations such as "C3." But when I ask people to imagine their workplace apart from money, no one has much to say. Money is too deeply a part of our life.

None of us can avoid money, but we can be much more conscious of how it functions in our lives. And in the workplace, one of the main uses of money is to measure time and to be traded for time.

TIME AND MONEY

The phrase "time is money" became popular, no doubt, during the heyday of "time-management studies," when it was an original insight about the relationship of efficiency to profit. No other phrase so succinctly describes how money alters our perceptions of ourselves and others once we step into the workplace. In this sense, work is an exchange of time for money. You give time, and your employer gives you money.

This implies that time is something that belongs to you, a possession of value that you can exchange for money by "spending" time at work. Employers define certain activities, such as making personal calls, as ones to be done on your "own" time versus the company's time. Perhaps that was what was so striking about my own transition from the monastery to the office. In the monastery time doesn't belong to anyone. It is something to be shared.

Now it may be clearer why the religious teachers of old all agreed that there was something corrosive about money. Saint Paul didn't say "Money is the root of all evil," although that is how the biblical passage is often misquoted; he said "the love of money." It is the way that money alters our state of mind, our sense of time, our sense of who we are and who others are, that is the problem. It is the love, the attachment to money, that drains our soul.

Time is life. We have time, because we are alive, because we exist in this world. When we die, we are out of time. Time ceases for us. Time, like life itself, is a gift. It comes to us freely, simply because we are here. Time is central to the spiritual inquiry, to the fundamental questions: Who am I? Why am I here? Time embraces these questions. It gives them depth and breadth.

One of the effects of formal meditation practice is the way that it expands our sense of time. Particularly during long meditation retreats, time becomes much more vivid, more palpable, more liquid. I often use the phrase "thick time" to describe this phenomenon. At work we experience time as thin—rushed, hurried, noisy, distracted. Following our breathing, minute by minute, hour by hour, time becomes neither slow nor fast. Time reverts to just what it is—

breath, heartbeat, birdsong, sunlight imperceptibly traveling across the rug. Time simply holds and contains us.

It may be helpful to add to our meditation on money an awareness of the breath. As we stare at the one- and the hundred-dollar bills, feel the breath going in and out. This is time, and the bills are money. Are they the same or different? Which one is a more accurate measure of true worth?

VALUE

Do you remember Harry Roberts's story in chapter 2 about his spiritual teacher sewing the ceremonial headdress? Let's revisit that story in more detail.

The story is about Robert, Harry's uncle and teacher, who was laboriously making a headdress for a ceremonial dance. Harry watched as his uncle took apart a section he had just spent twenty minutes sewing together. "Why are you taking it apart?" Harry asked. "The dance is at night. Nobody will see it. Who will know?"

"I will know," Robert replied.

This story is full of important truths about time, money, and value. Its context is a traditional, premodern society, one governed by ritual, custom, and the importance of character and personal relationships.

Robert was doing important work, but he was not getting paid for it. What's more, no one, except his young nephew Harry, was watching him do it. He could have done the task in the most expeditious way, thus saving time. But that would imply that time had some kind of quantifiable value and that saving time was important.

But saving time was not important to Robert at all; neither was producing a headdress that was only adequate the important thing. The important thing was his own internal sense of quality and his own state of mind. To Robert, the gift that he was going to bring to the ceremonial dance was not the headdress at all. It was what he had crafted inside himself, a standard of excellence, sincerity, and quality known only to him, that was the true gift. If he were to have gone to the ceremony with a headdress that to everyone else looked fine, but which he knew was not the best he could do, he would be ashamed. He would not want anyone at the ceremony to see him like that.

Robert lived in a culture where it was clearly understood that our state of mind is not only important but also real and tangible. That was what Robert meant when he said, "I will know." He meant that because he would notice, everyone would know.

This way of looking at the world is very different from our modern notions of value, money, and time.

Suppose a tourist had happened by Robert's house and had seen the headdress hanging outside on the front porch. And suppose the tourist encountered Robert and offered to buy the headdress.

Robert would have replied, "This headdress is not for sale. It's a ceremonial headdress."

But the tourist might have insisted. "Tell me how many hours you worked on it. I don't want to cheat you. I'll pay you fair value for the hours you put in. After all, time is money."

It would have been difficult for Robert to explain to the tourist that the value of the headdress didn't translate into hours or money. The value of the headdress was connected to the bonding together of the whole community, to Robert's place as an honored elder in that community, to the mutual trust that the tribe's ceremonies helped to cement.

Let's contrast Harry Roberts's story with one from the modern workplace. Jean was a departmental manager in a large investment firm. For the last two years, ever since a merger had forced many layoffs, Jean's job had been quite stressful. Before the merger she had a staff of forty-five, but now she had fewer than thirty, and the workload was, if anything, greater than before. It seemed to Jean that her job consisted mainly of listening to her subordinates' endless complaints. Though their frustration was legitimate, there was little Jean could do about it.

One day Charles, Jean's boss, called her into his office. "Jean, I know how frustrating the last year has been for you and your team, and I want you to know what a good job you've done and how much the firm appreciates your effort. I found some money in the budget, and I'm going to give you a five-thousand-dollar year-end bonus."

For the next few weeks, Jean felt as though she were walking on air. At last her hard work had been recognized. The end of the fiscal year was only a few weeks away. Jean spent the remaining weeks planning how she was going to use the money.

When she opened her year-end check she was surprised to see that the bonus was only thirty-two hundred dollars. "Oh, yes," Charles said, when she asked him about it, "they cut my budget at the last minute. You know how it is. I did the best I could."

Jean had a friend in the accounting department, and she couldn't resist. She asked her friend to check the departmental budget. "No cuts that I can see," her friend reported back. "Charles must have used the money for something else."

Jean's earlier euphoria now turned to anger. It was not the short-fall that disturbed her. The difference was only eighteen hundred dollars, after all, and she hadn't been expecting any bonus at all. It was what the shortfall implied about Charles's praise. It felt to Jean that Charles's acknowledgment wasn't wholehearted but calculated. Jean now wondered if the bonus was really in recognition of her effort or only to take the edge off her frustration.

She almost wished Charles hadn't given her any bonus at all. In the end, she didn't feel more valued but instead devalued.

Who knows if her assumptions about Charles were valid? Maybe he did sincerely wish to reward her and had a good reason for using some of the money elsewhere. Jean would never know, because she could not confront Charles about the matter without compromising her friend's confidence. So instead of feeling motivated and re-warded, Jean felt bitter. Instead of becoming closer to her boss, she felt more distant.

The lesson of this story is that even in the most money-oriented workplace, money is not the reward that counts the most. In this case, it was supposed to represent acknowledgment, but because of a subtle shift in the way it was tendered, it failed in that mission. Just as the tourist could not give Robert enough money to compensate him for the headdress, Charles's lack of straightforwardness and sincerity sapped the intended meaning out of Jean's bonus. I know of one company where bonuses went up from year to year and the cynical employees complained to one another, "The boss doesn't really appreciate us. He's just trying to buy our loyalty." The boss couldn't understand it. "I gave them more this year than last!" He didn't understand that, in the end, it isn't just the money but the intention that counts.

WORK FOR ITS OWN SAKE

I mentioned in the introduction to this section that not all work is for pay. We volunteer at the local convalescent home or soup kitchen, we spend hours in our home workshop pursuing our hobby, we spend the weekend painting the living room. All of us have experienced the liberation that comes when we can work without any thought of pay.

But what about our day job? Is there any way to bring that spirit into our actual workplace? To find small ways to work not for pay but for the sake of the work itself? If you like your job, if it satisfies and fulfills you, undoubtedly there are moments when you become so absorbed in your work, so inspired by it, that time opens up, becomes spacious and liquid, and you and the work become one.

But even when that is not the case, there may be opportunities to contribute work that is outside the time-money equation.

For example, consider the snack kitchen at work.

If you have no problem at all keeping your snack kitchen clean, then I want to come work with you, because you must work in heaven! At the company I used to work for, I tried everything—humorous signs, shame, hiding the cups. I made one sign that said, "We have just purchased a set of coffee cups that automatically wash themselves and put themselves away. It is an astonishing new invention, but they are on backorder, and until they arrive, will everyone wash and put away their own cup?"

People thought that was amusing, but it didn't change anyone's behavior.

I tried washing them myself, whenever I saw the sink filling up. This was not because I wanted to be a hero. In fact, I was, from time to time, one of the dirty-cup offenders. But I saw some of the data entry clerks—women—washing up after everyone else, and it made me feel guilty that they, who were paid much less than I was, found the time to do this and I could not.

In the Buddhist monastery, cleaning up was second nature. All the paths were neatly swept. The kitchen was spotless. That was how we spent our time—putting the kind of care and attention into the small details of life that no business could ever afford to pay us to do.

In the monastery, time is not money. Time is an opportunity for spiritual growth. In fact, we spent several hours each day sitting motionless on a cushion, facing a wall. What, in business terms, could be more unproductive than that, all of us highly educated people sitting in the darkness and the cold, doing nothing whatsoever?

Harry's uncle Robert would have understood. In his culture, this practice would have made complete sense. We were working on our inner life, our state of mind, our character. For someone like Robert, that was the whole point of living.

Travis was the senior worker in a plumbing firm that had an owner and five employees. Because growth depended on each employee's bringing in new business, the owner decided at one point to pay a commission for each new client an employee brought in. Travis, already the most highly paid as well as the most personable worker, quickly became the top commission earner, but after a few months he began to feel uncomfortable with the new arrangement. He approached his boss and suggested that all the commissions be put into a pool to be shared equally by all the employees. His boss was surprised. "That's going to be less money for you," he said. "I know," said Travis. "But the feeling among us has changed. We're not cooperating the way we used to. There's some tension." The boss talked it over with the other employees, and they all agreed.

"How much money did you lose when all the commissions were pooled?" I asked Travis when he told me this story.

"It's hard to say," Travis replied. "At first I lost a bit, but over time I think the newer plumbers worked harder to get new clients. In the long run, I probably didn't lose anything. I might have even gained a little."

"Why did you do it?" I asked.

"Under the old system, I didn't like how I felt on the job," Travis explained. "I'm the senior person in the firm. I had to be able to feel comfortable looking the other guys in the eye every day."

Not every workplace provides the kind of opportunity to express your convictions and character the way Travis did. But are there less dramatic ways you can express yourself in your own job?

If a coworker is having trouble with her workload, can you volunteer to help? If the receptionist forgot to put out the mail pouch, can you take the time to do it for him? If your workday ends at five, can you stay on an extra ten minutes sometimes, perhaps working on the part of your job that is most pleasing to you? And can you do these things not because you are hoping your boss will notice, or because you are bucking for a promotion, but because it helps to separate money from time and to give you the sense that regardless of how much or how little you are being paid, your time is your own, your greatest treasure?

From the perspective of "time is money," no one is paying you to do these things. You are busy. They don't pay you enough for the job you do, much less for something extra. Why bother?

Harry's uncle has the answer for you: "Because you will notice."

When you do something to satisfy your own state of mind, it is not just for yourself. Your state of mind is real, it is tangible, it affects others. It is nice for the next person to visit a clean snack kitchen, but what is even more important is for that person to feel your shining mind.

When you can find ways to slip out of "time is money" for just a few moments and enter into an activity that seems to provide you with nothing in return, then you have struck a secret blow for a different kind of human equation, the one that says "time is spirit" or "time is love."

Practices for Money and Time

- Gaze fixedly at a large-denomination bill, long enough to see it freshly, as though for the first time. What is it? What is your relationship to it?

- Sit quietly and attend to your breathing. Can you feel a change in your sense of time?

- Find a way to separate time from money at work. Do something outside your job description. How does it feel? What is different?

A pology and forgiveness go together. Typically, one follows the other. I apologize to you, and you forgive me. Apology and forgiveness have become something of a neglected art in today's fast-paced world. In the workplace, especially, petty irritations and hurts often cry out for resolution. Especially in larger companies, intrigue, deception, and malicious gossip are all too common.

My good friend Sylvia Boorstein, while reading this chapter, shared with me "the nine

words that would change the world," which she learned from Rabbi David Zeller. The nine words are "I'm sorry. I made a mistake. Please forgive me."

If we all made it a point to practice some form of these nine words, so that they dwelled in our heart, I have no doubt that it would indeed begin to change the world. There is an intimacy and magnetism to apology and forgiveness that breaks down the barriers between people and draws them closer. That intimacy is difficult to regain in the modern workplace, where strangers are often thrust together in impersonal cubicles. But through our spiritual intention and sustained effort, each of us can bring that spirit back to life.

The energy of apology and forgiveness may seem at first blush to belong in the Cool

I'm sorry. I made a mistake. Please forgive me.

nine words that could change the world

Positive realm of calm and ease. Certainly the release of tension that occurs when apology is answered with forgiveness may be a great relief. But the act of apology itself is a high-energy affair. Sometimes apology can have as much heat as anger.

By way of illustration, let me tell you about another of my favorite movies, *Rickshaw Man,* which features Matsu, a rickshaw driver in turn-of-the-century Japan. In the opening scene, Matsu wants to attend a performance of the local theater. Tradition allowed rickshaw drivers to attend such events for free. But when Matsu steps up to the ticket booth, expecting to be waved in, the theater manager refuses to honor the tradition. Matsu angrily returns with a ticket, enters the theater, and proceeds to tear the place up. He starts a fire, throws food, and gets into a fight, bringing the performance to a halt.

The distraught theater manager calls in the local "boss," a prominent citizen, to mediate the dispute. The boss, seated with dignity on a straw mat, listens patiently to both sides of the story. He hears Matsu's impassioned, angry defense of the rickshaw driver's traditional rights, as well as the theater manager's description of Matsu's misbehavior. The boss patiently explains to Matsu that while his feelings may have been justified, his behavior was upsetting to many people. He then turns to the theater manager and upbraids him for refusing to honor the tradition.

Matsu, a simple, honest man, screws up his forehead as he listens to the boss's words and realizes the full implications of what he has done. Turning his whole body to face the theater manager, he bows to the floor and shouts out in a husky voice, "I'm sorry!"

The manager, greatly relieved, replies, "You are forgiven."

The boss is deeply impressed with Matsu's actions. "You are the most straightforward man I have ever met," he exclaims. "Your words as good as erased your actions."

This story is a vivid illustration of the transformation of energy from the hot, negative anger of Matsu and the theater manager to the equally hot but positive "I'm sorry!" that Matsu shouts out with his head touching the ground.

Can you imagine a comparable scene occurring in your workplace? Are you Matsu the rickshaw man, or are you the theater manager? Or perhaps you are the boss! I once knew a warehouse worker who was offended by what he perceived to be a racial slur uttered by his boss. He was in the process of scattering a week's supply of styrofoam peanuts all over the floor when his boss, having heard from another worker about the cause of his upset, confronted him.

"I'm sorry, man. I didn't mean it the way you thought. I really didn't."

The worker glared at him for a while and then understood that the apology was sincere. "Okay," he said. The two of them spent the next half hour cleaning up the styrofoam together.

Can you imagine the situation if the boss had not apologized, and the two of them continued to come to work day after day with that unresolved tension between them? It is one thing not to forgive the rude driver who cuts you off on the freeway. You will never see him again. But we spend more time with our workmates than we do with anyone else, even our family. Unresolved conflicts at work are an enormous drain. They have a detrimental effect on everyone, and sometimes they can boil over and explode.

PRACTICING APOLOGY

A sincere apology can have enormous power. Not too many years ago, the president of the United States offered an apology to all the Japanese Americans interned during World War II. Each of them also got around twenty thousand dollars, but when the press interviewed some of the aging internees, they all said the apology, coming from the president himself, was more important to them than the money.

Can you think of opportunities in your workplace where an apology would help? It is human nature to imagine that your hurts are more in need of salving than others' wounds. We also tend to think that apology is a sign of weakness, that it makes us lower than the other person. "Me apologize to him? Never! He's the one who should apologize."

In fact, to apologize is an act of strength. To apologize means that you are strong enough to give something up, to move some positive energy out of your domain and toward someone else. Think of how the boss reacted when he observed Matsu's apology: "You are the most straightforward man I have ever met." Matsu did not hedge— "I'll apologize if he apologizes," or "Yes, I was wrong, but it's fifty-fifty here." He just went all the way, without thinking about whether the ledger of blame was balanced.

It is easy to apologize conditionally, or strategically, when we think there is something to gain. It is very different to apologize unconditionally, simply as a way to transform the energy of the situation. That kind of apology is more than just etiquette; it is a genuine spiritual practice. I read recently that Joe Montana, who for so many years was the quarterback for the San Francisco 49ers, would often take the blame for others' mistakes. If the center fumbled the snap, Joe would tell the coach, "It was me. I blew it." That was one reason he was such a respected team leader.

Think now about just one situation in the workplace for which you could offer an unconditional apology. There's no need to make long lists. One is enough. Do you feel some uneasiness, a sense that the apology would be hard, or not really warranted? Good! That's exactly the kind of apology we are looking for.

Now do it, simply as an experiment. One small apology won't hurt you or affect your hard-won status on the job as somebody of consequence, somebody to be reckoned with. In fact, if that is your reputation already, your apology will have considerable power. You might even try apologizing to somebody whom you know really ought to be apologizing to you. Remember Joe Montana: "It was me. I blew it." I have little doubt that everyone on the team, including the coach, knew what had really happened. I'd also guess that the center who blew the snap was deeply motivated not to let Joe down again.

PRACTICING FORGIVENESS

Like most other religions, Buddhism recognizes the importance of forgiveness and offers an extensive body of practices to develop the forgiving spirit. These practices recognize that before we can truly forgive another person, we need to know how to forgive ourselves. This approach is quite practical. It recognizes that it is easier to change ourselves than to change someone else. And if we are harsh and unforgiving of our own shortcomings, how can we be generous with the faults of others?

What allows us to forgive others is the ability to see their faults as our own, to identify with them enough to get inside their skin, to feel what they feel, to see what they see. When the boss in *Rickshaw Man* got the theater manager to really see his behavior through Matsu's eyes, the manager immediately forgave Matsu. For a moment, he became Matsu.

When someone makes a cutting remark at work, when our boss dismisses our carefully prepared proposal with a wave of her hand, when our best friend reveals a confidence to a superior and puts our career at risk, how can we avoid feeling hurt and vengeful? Only if we acknowledge forthrightly that we ourselves are not above such things, that in another time and another place we might have done the same, that all of us are flawed and often act less than our best— only then can we find it in our heart to forgive.

That is why Buddhism says: Begin with yourself. Know yourself thoroughly enough to be able to say "It is all right. I can forgive myself and accept myself for who I am."

Forgiveness is not just an intellectual exercise. It is physical, and its center is the heart. We have many phrases in our language that refer to the heart: "brokenhearted," "her heart sank," "his heart was in his throat," "bighearted." These are not just figures of speech. They describe actual sensations. Forgiveness is a sensation too. When it is real, it releases a flood of physical feeling, an energy flow within ourselves, and between us and our adversary. These sensations are an important part of the practice of forgiveness.

The Friend in the Heart meditation that follows is one way to make forgiveness physical, to give it a home not just in your head, as an idea, but in your body, in your heart. When the moment of forgiveness is upon us, when we are face-to-face with the one who hurt us, we need more than just the right words. We need to engage all our senses and all our feeling. We need to find our own Voice of Truth and express it in such a way that our adversary can feel it and accept it.

Professional singers learn that there are many places in the body to put the voice. High notes vibrate in the top of the head. Middle notes sound in the chest. And low notes are produced in the stomach, or even the pelvis or thighs. A singer learns that it is not just the vocal cords that sing but the whole body. Children are quite aware of this difference. When parents scold them and make them apologize, they have a way of whining "Sorr-e-e-e!" that clearly indicates they don't mean it. We adults are more subtle, but we know how to do this too.

A FRIEND IN THE HEART

To begin the practice, settle yourself in a comfortable sitting posture, either cross-legged on a cushion or in a chair. Now reach up and touch the area below your breastbone. Do you feel a subtle sensation of warmth? This feeling is not your physical heart but your wisdom or spiritual heart.

Now give this area under your breastbone a name: the word *friend.* As you breathe in, repeat the word silently to yourself, but from your chest, as though a little voice had piped up there, saying the word. Put that word into the heart territory. Picture it floating inside your chest. As you breathe in, let the voice in your chest whisper it silently.

Now expand the voice. Have it say "Best Friend."

Best friend. What do those words evoke for you? What is the sensation that you feel in the heart when you silently say them? Think about your best friend. Think of how you feel when you are together. Think of what you would do for that person, how you would help her and care for her. Perhaps your best friend is also your spouse or partner. We have such good feelings about our best friends. We appreciate their strengths, we overlook their faults, we are "all the way for them," as Harry Roberts used to say.

Can you take all those feelings, gather them up into a bouquet, and offer them to yourself?

What do you feel?

Perhaps you feel a bit odd. Such a practice can feel odd at first. But that sense of odd is itself a testament to the fact that the practice reaches you. The part of you that says "odd" is holding back, skeptical, unwilling to give up the status quo. But it is still responding.

As you go through your workday, three or four times a day, lean back in your chair, take a deep breath, and recollect the practice of the Friend in the Heart. Rekindle that sensation, and let your heart voice whisper its word in your chest.

"Friend."

"Best Friend."

This is particularly helpful when the next kernel on your string of popcorn has turned red, when things are not going well, when you have just made a mistake or been criticized. What would your best friend do if she could suddenly materialize before you? She would comfort you, reassure you, forgive you.

Can you do that for yourself?

FORGIVE YOURSELF

Now that you are on your way to becoming your own best friend, see if you can find something specific about yourself that needs forgiveness. Perhaps you have treated someone badly at work. Perhaps you have been trying, and failing, to improve some damaging habit. Or, most commonly of all, perhaps you are not taking good care of yourself, not exercising, not eating well, not balancing your work life with family and personal interests.

See if you can capture that critical feeling as though trapping an insect under a glass jar. Draw it back toward yourself and bring it into view. Now let the voice that is in your heart, the one that has been saying "Friend, Friend," extend itself to the buzzing beast.

Say "Friend."

It is not enough just to say the words, just to whisper them to yourself. It is important to actually feel the sensation and feeling of the words in your heart, just as you would feel a vibration in your throat if you were to say them aloud. From a spiritual perspective, the heart is an organ of speech. It has its own voice and life.

Say "Forgive."

"I forgive myself. It is all right."

"I forgive myself for criticizing my coworker too harshly. It is all right. I can make a mistake. I will try to do better next time."

Can you feel it in your chest? Is your pulse picking it up and carrying it around your whole body along with your breath and your blood?

In group therapy sessions, sometimes the therapist will have everyone in the group focus on one person, and each one will tell that person the same message: "It is all right. We forgive you." I have listened while ten or twelve people in turn said this to me. It is a strange experience. The first four or five times the words are repeated, the message remains abstract. It reaches the ears and the brain, but it doesn't really sink in. But after the seventh or eighth time, something shifts. Now it is not just the brain that is getting the message but the heart. We actually feel something.

This is how real forgiveness can have the power to release you.

FORGIVE ANOTHER

How do you feel about forgiving yourself? Do you really feel forgiven? Can you forgive another person with the same sincerity?

What about an adversary? Sit quietly, close your eyes, and imagine that your adversary is sitting in front of you, facing you. Try to bring up the feelings you have about that person, the irritation, annoyance, or anger.

Now, with your eyes still closed, imagine a voice in your heart awakening and speaking the word: "Forgive."

How does your feeling about your adversary change?

Do you feel resistance? Does the message come from your brain, not your heart? Are you like I was, sitting in the center of the circle, listening to one person after another say "You are all right," but not quite believing it?

Say it again. "Forgive." And again.

See how long it takes, how many repetitions are necessary, before something starts to move in the heart, before the body joins with the words and starts to awaken with an energy you can feel.

If it doesn't seem to be working, no matter how many times you repeat the word, then try a different approach. Imagine that the chair in which your imaginary adversary has been sitting becomes suddenly empty, and a new person sits down in it—you! Now you yourself are the adversary. Be honest with yourself. Have you ever behaved in the same way as your adversary has? Can you imagine doing to someone else what your adversary has done to you?

If we are honest, we may discover that what annoys us most about an adversary is something that we have a tendency to do ourselves. This fact draws on an interesting psychological and spiritual truth—what irks us in another is often a reflection of what we cannot accept in ourselves. For example, I don't like to be interrupted. But being quick and impulsive by temperament, I have a tendency to interrupt others! When someone interrupts me, it is like a mirror image of my own shortcoming. When we realize how much these personal shadows affect our irritations with others, we can further appreciate the connection between forgiving ourselves and forgiving another.

Now try repeating the words again: "I forgive." This time it is not someone else you are forgiving, not the one who hurt you, but you yourself, who are your own best friend.

Can you do it?

FORGIVENESS IN THE WORKPLACE

Here is a specific example of how such a practice might be used in the workplace. Randy worked in a large healthcare organization. He considered himself to be an honest, hardworking soul, and it bothered him that many of his coworkers were, as he termed them, "sluffoffs," just putting in their time. As one colleague confided to him over coffee one day, "This job is awful, isn't it? The only reason I'm here is for the benefits."

The benefits were indeed good, including a generous pension plan, but Randy could not shake his feeling of annoyance, which over time turned to real anger, toward his cynical coworkers. There was one fellow in particular, a middle-aged supervisor named Carl, who rarely spoke. It was well known in the department that he was just marking time until his retirement in two years. Randy often ran into Carl in the elevator first thing in the morning. Every time he saw Carl, Randy greeted him with a cheery "Good morning! How are you doing?" But Carl would only mumble and avert his eyes.

Randy found this reaction infuriating. When he recounted the situation to members of our workshop, several people suggested he leave Carl alone. "Maybe the poor guy just doesn't want to talk," one said.

"What are you trying to accomplish?" I asked Randy.

"I just want him to respond!" Randy replied heatedly. "He's like a zombie. They're all zombies!"

A bit later in the session, we practiced the Friend in the Heart meditation I described earlier. After we were finished, Randy raised his hand. "What if you don't feel particularly friendly toward yourself?" he asked.

"That's one purpose of the meditation," I replied. "To bring that feeling up, so that we are aware of it. If we can't be friendly with ourselves, it's hard to extend that feeling to anyone else."

The next week, Randy reported that instead of trying to push Carl to respond in the elevator, he had just practiced the Friend in the Heart meditation while they rode up together.

"Did anything change?" I asked.

"Well, Carl didn't change, if that's what you mean," Randy said. "As much of a zombie as ever." Randy paused. "But I think he didn't bug me quite as much."

I didn't say so, but I would guess that for Randy, Carl represented some part of himself that he didn't like and couldn't accept. To work on his feeling about Carl, Randy really needed to work on his feeling about Randy!

Sometimes people will object, "So you're saying it's all our problem? That we should blame ourselves rather than the bad work situation?"

No, I'm not saying that. We should work on both. Workers still need to bargain with management and, if necessary, go on strike. Victims of mistreatment need to seek redress, in the courts if necessary. But apart from those practical steps, which may take a long time and may or may not be successful, we dwell in the center of our own experience and have access to that center any time we choose. In Randy's case, I think probably some part of him wanted to sluff off too. After all, his coworkers were getting away with it! But he didn't like that part of himself. He couldn't be friendly with it. He wanted to see himself only as a good person, a good worker, perhaps even a superior worker.

We human beings all want pretty much the same things. We all have similar bad habits and negative tendencies. Those faults give us a strong capacity to forgive and are the reason why forgiveness can be so effective.

In closing, remember the nine words that could change the world—or if not the world, at least ourselves.

"I'm sorry. I made a mistake. Please forgive me."

Nine words, but they encompass so much.

PRACTICES FOR FORGIVENESS

- Sit quietly and put the word "Friend" in your heart. Can you feel an actual sensation?

- Visualize your adversary sitting in a chair before you. Imagine saying the words "I forgive."

- As an experiment, try apologizing to someone at work. What happens? What changes?

In my workshops, it is not uncommon, during the initial introductions, for a person to say, "I used to be a vice president for Corporation X, but I got so fed up with the politics and backbiting that I started my own business, and now I do consulting out of my spare bedroom."

Much of this book is about making the best of your work situation by remembering that you are the boss of your inner life. But what if that isn't enough? It may not be enough for you to be the boss of your inner

life; you may need to be the boss of your outer one too, or at least to move to a different, more supportive work situation.

But before you march in and give the tell-off-the-boss speech—stop! Reread the chapter on Ambition, and then take another look at the chapter on Worry. And don't forget the chapter on Failure! You can't assume that everything will go well. A more supportive job, one that is more in tune with your own character and values, may not pay as well as your current position. There are risks, especially if you imagine working for yourself or starting your own business. Going solo is not for everyone. But as the following example demonstrates, if striking out on your own *is* the right thing for you, the rewards in inner satisfaction, self-esteem, and autonomy can outweigh a reduction in income.

To be successful at quitting as a spiritual practice, we need to go "outside the box."

QUITTING THE RAT RACE

Janice was one of those who raised her hand when I asked, "Who here has tried 'quitting as a spiritual practice'?" Janice used to be an accountant and administrative manager for a law firm where the business culture was aggressive, brash, and loud. Partners were expected to bring in large amounts of new business every year, or else they were not partners for long. Much of the strain of this work style fell on Janice, who, in addition to her official duties, was the managing partner's chief troubleshooter, the one responsible for putting out fires, calming the waters, and keeping everything rolling.

Janice was often overwhelmed by the demands on her time and energy, especially because she was also pursuing a course of yoga training in the evenings. The way she coped was to silently repeat to herself, whenever she could, the phrase "I am peace. I am peace." She wasn't trying to affect anyone else, just to calm her own state of mind, but her effort did seem to have an outward effect. Once, her boss even stopped in mid-tirade to say to her, "What are you doing to me!" Even so, eventually she left that job to take up a career as a yoga instructor.

Janice came up with her own spiritual practice, a self-mantra that not only helped her manage her own state of mind but also had some transformative effect on others. But it was not enough. The ultimate effect of the practice was to give her enough strength and confidence to leave. She took a big pay cut and had to do freelance accounting in addition to her yoga teaching to support herself. Yoga wasn't nearly as lucrative as law administration, but it was much more satisfying personally.

WHEN YOU KNOW IT'S TIME TO GO

When is quitting your job the right thing to do—spiritually, emotionally, and financially—and when is it rash and ill advised? You don't want to be like Jason in chapter 11, whose quitting led to personal and financial disaster. And yet you can't always replicate the success of Janice, who was lucky to have an alternate skill that was more satisfying.

Knowing when to stay at your job and when to go is one of those major life decisions, like choosing a college, getting married, or planning to have children, for which there is no set formula or easy answer. However, several of the practices we have already covered can be useful in planning the move and making the decision.

The practice of Truthful Feeling, which we explored in chapter 11, is often the first step. When you keep asking "How do I feel about my job right now?" and find that the reply is "Not so good," that is an answer worth paying attention to. The thought of quitting your job rarely arrives fully formed but typically begins with a nagging feeling that you may not acknowledge or recognize for a while. By the time you are ready to begin asking the question in earnest, you may have been mulling it over in a preconscious form for some time.

The practice of being your own best friend, which we covered in the previous chapter, is essential. The whole thrust of such a major decision is to take better care of yourself, to put your own ideals and values above riches, ambition, status, glamour, and the perceptions and opinions of others. You even have to face the sense of loss that will come if you decide to leave.

That loss is real. When Janice announced that she was leaving, her whole firm went into mourning. Her boss took her aside, pleaded with her to stay, and even offered her a big raise. Several of the associates confided to her privately that without her, they did not know if they could stay long enough to make partner. That was the hardest part for her, the sense that she was letting her colleagues down. She did have second thoughts but, in the end, decided that she had to put her own needs first.

THE INNER AND OUTER ENTREPRENEUR

Whether or not you are planning to become self-employed or just to find another occupation, changing jobs is an act of entrepreneurship. Even if all this means is that you're going to career counseling, updating your résumé, or scouring the want ads, you have already begun working for yourself.

I did not start my present business until I was forty-six years old. For that matter, I was thirty-five before I got my first job in the profit sector. But when I did strike out on my own, I discovered two things. First, I liked being my own boss. It suited me better than taking orders from someone else. And second, to my surprise, I actually had some talent as an entrepreneur. I'm not quite sure why. Some people say entrepreneurs are born, not made. I certainly didn't learn it in school. (I was a music and philosophy major!) Recently, I've concluded some of these skills were honed during my years as a monk, when I spent much of the day sitting on a cushion facing a wall. Strange as it may sound, there is an entrepreneurial quality to meditation!

Most people begin a formal spiritual practice by expecting to be told what to do, just as they would be on a regular job. They receive instruction and try to follow the directions. One of the common questions beginners ask is "Am I doing it right?" The whole process seems to be about doing things a certain way. It is true that in Buddhist monastic life there are rules for everything: for entering the meditation hall, for bowing, for taking a bath, for eating and cooking. Of course, the rules aren't arbitrary. They help us to pay attention, to show respect, to be aware and awake. Rules are not unique to Buddhism. The Bible is full of rules. The Talmud and the Koran both have traditions of rule and custom that the faithful are expected to follow.

But at a certain point we come to the realization that the rules are there to enable us to know ourselves. At that point we must strike out on our own and make the rules not something to follow from outside but something that we express from inside. In order to make the spiritual tradition our own, we need to become entrepreneurs of the spirit.

One of the primary characteristics of any entrepreneur is this willingness to go "outside the box," to envision that which is not yet visible. An American Buddhist teacher once said to me, "The way I identify potential teacher candidates is to look for students who are a bit rebellious, who don't do exactly what the tradition says, or what I say. But of course I can't tell them so in advance. They have to figure it out for themselves."

That is one quality we need to cultivate to be successful at quitting as a spiritual practice. We need to go "outside the box." We need to see ourselves not as we are today but as we might be tomorrow. We need to take inventory of our skills and talents and assess which of them might be a livelihood. We need to correlate what we are good at with what fulfills us.

RAISE THE QUESTION: AM I READY?

If you already have a good job, one that pays the bills and keeps a roof over your head, then one good piece of advice is: Take your time! Don't rush. Don't act from emotion, as Jason did in chapter 11, or from exhaustion. If your job has been frustrating and difficult for months or years, a few more months won't make a huge difference. Give yourself time to picture the whole process. Above all, live with the question: Am I ready?

Put that question, or one like it, into your heart and call it forth every day. Breathe it, walk it, eat it, and sleep it. Be prepared for all possible answers. No! I am not ready. I will never be ready (the voice of fear). Yes! I will do it today! (the voice of confidence). I don't even know what I want (the voice of confusion). These voices are all you. Respect them all. Don't favor one over the other. Let them all speak, until, over time, one begins to prevail. Remember the Voice of Truth, which we discussed in chapter 6? If you're not sure which of your many voices is the true one, then keep listening. If no voice emerges as the one to honor, then in all likelihood you are not ready. Keep working and keep listening.

How will you know when the voice is true? In thinking back on my own experience of starting a business, there was no one moment when I jumped out of bed in the morning and thought, "Yes! This is it!" For me, the decision worked in the other direction. After I had already begun developing a product in the evenings and getting a feel for how it was to be on my own, a day came when I suddenly realized I was comfortable with what I was doing. Being on my own suited me.

MAKE A PLAN

It goes without saying that you should make a plan. This includes a financial plan, an action plan (networking, contacts, a business plan if you are starting your own enterprise), and a "friends, family, and loved ones" plan. There are many books on the business shelf of your local bookstore that will help you with the practical details. But spiritual preparation is equally important. Try to visualize, with each step of your transition, how you are likely to feel. Include exhilaration, terror, worry, nagging doubt, and a host of other twists and turns of this roller-coaster ride. Visualize these emotions in advance. Practice your reaction.

In the early days of my own business, worry was my constant companion. As I have said before, I found worry to be quite useful. Worry helped me plan. It tended to arise whenever I lacked a plan and helped point me to the places where I needed one. Once I got accustomed to the fact that worry was going to be my close companion whether I wanted it to be or not, it became my lodestone, pointing me in the direction I needed to go.

One time, in the early days of my business, I was down to my last few weeks of cash. I had two sales pending, but neither one seemed likely to close soon. My credit lines and credit cards were already maxed out. In the vernacular of business start-ups, I was "scraping bottom." I took this problem to bed with me every night and confronted it when I got up every morning. There was no escaping it. After two weeks of this, I woke up in the middle of the night and thought, "I already have a large client. They're happy with the product. I could ask them for their next year's maintenance fees in advance." Would they agree? Sure enough, when I asked them, they were happy to do it. That payment got me through. Telling the story now, it seems like such an obvious solution, but at the time it was a real breakthrough for me to realize that I had established enough credibility with my existing customers to ask for, and get, help.

That is an example of a plan that worked. I also explored many blind alleys, many seemingly promising schemes that ended up going nowhere. I juggled several plans—I had one plan if my bank account ran out before the next revenue check, another if a big check came in. As a process, planning is not as orderly as it seems on paper. The reality is more messy and cluttered.

SEEK ADVICE

My wife and I married young. She was twenty-two, and I was one month shy of twenty. We sought the advice of a Unitarian minister whose job it was to advise other ministers. Since we both taught Sunday school at the local Unitarian church, it seemed like a natural place to seek advice. The minister, who was supportive and helpful, acknowledged that we seemed to be levelheaded and deeply in love, but his final conclusion was that we were too young and should wait.

We checked with my parents. They said we were too young and should wait.

We checked with my wife's parents. Guess what they said?

So, after all that, we ignored everyone's advice and got married anyway. I'm happy to report that we just celebrated our thirty-first wedding anniversary. Unfortunately, the Unitarian minister we consulted got divorced the year after we spoke with him. A few years after that, my parents divorced too. I wish I could honestly say that the thought "I told you so!" never entered our heads.

That's one story about seeking advice. Here's another. In the early days of my software company, I consulted an industry expert about pricing. "Most of the companies in your industry are small," he said. "You should keep the price low. Grow your company on volume." For a while I tried his advice, but, as it turned out, our first few clients were large companies, for whom the risk and cost of a new product was more palatable. Their commitment to the product, and their success with it, helped establish the market price, which kept rising. Once the product was proven by the larger companies, smaller companies were willing to pay a higher price for it.

Listen to all the advice, but remember that other people are not you. The reason why you are contemplating this change is because of an inner voice that only you can hear. Don't be intimidated by their doubts or overly excited by their vicarious enthusiasm. Go back within yourself and continue to ask the question "Am I ready?"

WHAT IF YOU FAIL?

It is often said that what distinguishes the entrepreneur is a larger tolerance for failure. Thomas Edison tried thousands of combinations of materials before he was successful in inventing the lightbulb. Like most entrepreneurs, he didn't experience these disappointments as failures, but as clues on the road to success.

Whether your new venture is a new job or your own business, it may fail or go through a period where it appears as if it might fail. Your contingency planning should include this possibility. I have known several entrepreneurs who wrapped themselves in a cloak of invulnerability, thinking that failure was impossible for them. They are the ones who go off the deep end when real failure actually happens. Their self-image, their cardboard construct of confidence, doesn't hold up.

Don't go down that road. An old saying among career criminals goes "If you can't do the time, don't commit the crime." If you aren't prepared to fail, you'd better not take that first step into the unknown. Knowing that you can fail, and clearly understanding the danger signs that warn of failure, is the best way not to fail. That's the positive side of worry, as we discussed in chapter 5. Worry is about paying attention to the dangers that surround us.

NOTICE EVERYTHING

Once, when I and some other members of our Buddhist community were taking a walk with Harry Roberts, he suddenly stopped and held up his hand. "Hold it!" he said, pointing down at our feet. "That's yerba buena. It's a valuable medicine plant. Don't step on that. We should harvest it and dry it." We were oblivious to the significance of the plant, but Harry noticed it as he walked along. He was attentive to the opportunity around him.

Whenever you are starting something new, notice everything. You never know what may turn out to be important. Luck is a factor in all new things, but at least half of luck is paying attention, even to the most insignificant things. I once read that the man who invented Velcro got the idea from trying to clean burrs off his clothes after a hike in the woods. When he examined the burr closely, he saw how its structure allowed it to cling to fabric. How many millions of people have cleaned burrs off their clothes? Many indeed! And how many invented Velcro?

PATIENCE AND MORE PATIENCE

One mistake I made in starting my own business was underestimating the time required. The results I pictured at the end of the first year did come to pass, but not until the end of year two. I was prepared to work myself to the bone for two years, but I had to do it for three. Things take longer than we think.

Patience is an important spiritual virtue. In fact, in Buddhism, it has equal standing with meditation and wisdom. But the word *patience* implies something that is probably a bit too passive for what Buddhism means. In working our way through an important decision, we need acceptance, receptivity, and a willingness to stay with confusion and uncertainty. It isn't just waiting, it is working!

Here's a good test of your capacity for patience. When you feel that you are ready to make your move, when you feel as fully prepared as you will ever be, when all the signs are "go," then—stop!

Put it all aside, up on a shelf, and revisit that feeling in a week's or a month's time.

And if the opposite happens, if there is no sign of clarity anywhere on the horizon, then do the same—wait! What cosmic law says that the process will only take so long and no longer? Who told Edison that he would find the right combination of filament and coil in a thousand tries and not two thousand? (I believe it took him more than five thousand!) If you are still mulling over your decision, then something is driving you to keep at it. Honor that energy. It is your deeper life working its way up from the depths into the sunlight.

STAYING PUT

And if you decide, after all this, that the time is not right, and you should stay in your current situation, then good for you! The effort has not been in vain. Next year, or two years from now, who knows? Circumstances may change, and the decision that you set aside may reappear in a fresh suit of clothes.

Janice, the law administrator turned yoga teacher, came close to quitting her job several times. Once she even drafted her resignation letter on her home computer where no one in the office could see it. She worked on that letter for weeks. But it was another year before she finally printed it out and sent it. Having that letter in her home computer helped her stay put and recognize when the time was right.

HUMILITY

Quitting as a spiritual practice takes advantage of our freedom to choose, a freedom more available to the economically advantaged than the minimum-wage earner, for whom any job is a gift. So those of us who have the freedom to choose must remember to be grateful. All over the world, people lack this fundamental freedom. We have a responsibility to exercise this privilege responsibly, and with humility.

That is why, when the great moment finally comes, and you can finally give the tell-off-the-boss speech, be generous. Maybe that is not the right speech to give. You are now the strong one who had the will and the perseverance to map your own destiny. Maybe your boss, the one who has made your workdays so trying, has his own ambitions. Maybe all along he has envied you. We should be gracious in our good fortune. We never know when that generosity will be re-paid.

Good luck!

PRACTICES FOR QUITTING

- Ask yourself, "How do I feel about my job right now?" Ask every day.

- Raise the Question: "Am I ready?" Stay with the question and fol-low it as it changes. Honor all the various answers that arise.

- If you were to quit your job today, do you have a plan? If you don't, can you make a plan? Perhaps several plans?

- How can you seek others' advice without either blindly following it or rejecting those parts you do not want to hear?

- Imagine quitting your job and failing in your plan. What would you do? How would you feel?

- When is the last time something "lucky" happened to you? How much did you contribute to that event? How can you cultivate luck?

part five

ACCOMPLISHMENT

True accomplishment is not about winning,
acquiring, or being on top. It is about sharing,
giving, and including.

SUCCESS is the conventional goal of work life—to complete the project, to secure the promotion, to make the big sale, to improve profits. Conventional wisdom holds that success is what we all desire, and that when we are successful, we will be contented, relaxed, and calm. Of course, success is cause for celebration. And it often leads to feelings of contentment and ease, which are consistent with our characterization of this sector of the Energy Wheel as Cool Positive. However, in the work world, as well as in life, success can be fleeting. This year's profit is next year's loss. The promotion brings with it a host of new problems. The sought-after new client changes his mind.

From a spiritual standpoint, there is a different kind of success, one that does not come and go with the changing winds of the marketplace but stays with you because it is within you. This is Accomplishment.

Accomplishment is a matter of spirit, character, and even physiology. Scientists who have studied serotonin, a substance found in the brain, have discovered two complementary facts: Successful people have higher levels of serotonin, and high levels of serotonin help foster success. Even chimpanzees exhibit this chemical phenomenon; the dominant chimp has a serotonin-rich brain. A practical outcome of this research is the new generation of antidepressant drugs, which work partly by boosting serotonin levels. It seems that deep within our body there are processes at work that both support and reflect Accomplishment.

When human beings lived in small clans and communities, Accomplishment was clear and uncomplicated. A hunter who killed the bear and brought home the pelt was given a feast. Songs were sung, and for the rest of his days he would be known as Bearkiller. It is hard to kill a bear, and dangerous. It requires skill, fortitude, and luck. Not many people can do it. When you do, it is not just the animal you have slain but also your own fear, uncertainty, and doubt. You are changed, and you acquire inner power for both yourself and your community. Inner power is a topic we will be exploring in more detail later in this section.

In today's world, so much of what passes for outward success is, from a spiritual standpoint, rather hollow. Our society applauds wealth, fame, and celebrity, but as all of us who read *People* magazine understand, those things bring no guarantee of lasting happiness. We follow the personal crises of celebrities partly to satisfy ourselves that these paragons of success have no more handle on lasting happiness than we do—an observation that consoles us as we compare our modest station in life with theirs.

True Accomplishment is not about winning, acquiring, or being on top. It is about sharing, giving, and including. Is there room for that in our work? In today's workplace, the drive for ordinary success can sometimes actually get in the way of Accomplishment. The competitive nature of modern work ensures that where there are winners, there will be losers, and that success will often be measured in ways that hinder, even prevent, real Accomplishment from flourishing. Two familiar examples are sacrificing product quality for more profits and promoting a manager not because she manages well, but because she keeps costs down. Profit and lowered costs produce success. Product quality and good management are examples of Accomplishment. Even when Accomplishment comes, it is often unacknowledged by a workplace that doesn't recognize its value. The standard measures of workplace success—revenue growth, profit, market share, name brand recognition—miss more subtle accomplishments such as employee satisfaction, community involvement, minimizing pollution, and honesty.

Once after a lecture on this topic, a woman came up to me nearly in tears. She had worked for ten years as an elementary school teacher in a poor neighborhood. She was an excellent teacher and had the commendations to prove it. But not once in those ten years, she said, had anyone really acknowledged the difficulty of her work. If they had, it would have meant more to her than all her outward tokens of success. After ten years, she left teaching for good. She was back in school, training for another career. She knew that her Accomplishment was real. She could see it in the eyes of her students. But because the school system did not have a way to acknowledge what she had done, she did not have the energy to continue.

This section will explore ways to discover Accomplishment as well as how to manage conventional success, which changes, fades, and moves on. If we could rest on our laurels forever, like the gods of Mount Olympus, how wonderful that would be! This deepest desire of human beings, to be happy and safe forever, is a double problem for us. Not only is such a state unattainable, it isn't even that enjoyable! The Greek gods weren't exactly happy. In fact, they acted much like the bored jet-setters of today. And the Buddha, who was born as a prince into luxury but left behind riches and power to become a wandering ascetic, based his whole spiritual teaching on the realization that even as a prince and king he could not find lasting happiness.

Knowing how to manage your own success gracefully—with dignity, humility, good humor, and generosity—is a sign of wisdom. Even though outward success—a fancy job title, a fat paycheck—is fleeting and ephemeral, Accomplishment is not. Accomplishment is one of the few things in our unpredictable life that lasts, even after our death. Accomplishment allows us to look back when we are old and say, "I did that. I am happy for it. It helped. It made a difference."

Herb was a retired insurance executive in his eighties. Financially secure and still healthy, Herb should have been the exemplar of professional success. Outwardly he was, but when he looked back on his career, he did not feel any deep satisfaction. Instead he felt some regret. Insurance work had not given him a sense of Accomplishment.

One day, he received a letter from Arnold, a man who had worked for him decades before. Arnold was gay, and at that time prejudice against gays was strong. Although Arnold never revealed his secret to anyone at the insurance firm—to have done so might have meant dismissal—many of Arnold's superiors suspected the truth. As he was passed over for promotions, Arnold came to realize that the secret hand of prejudice was at work. Herb made it a point to take Arnold under his wing, to mentor him, and to see that he attained a position in the company commensurate with his talents. Herb had always believed that people should be treated fairly, regardless of their religion or personal life. He didn't feel that what he had done for Arnold was special.

When Herb opened Arnold's letter, he read that Arnold considered him one of the most important people in his life, the one who had made the most difference. Arnold's thanks to Herb was heartfelt. Herb was deeply moved by the letter. "That letter was probably the most important thing that ever happened to me in my job," he explained to me. "And I never knew until now." The letter was worth more than all of Herb's years of salary and bonuses, achievement medals and stock options, because it represented not just outward success but true Accomplishment.

It is by the grace of such reflections that we are able to look back on our life and say it was worthwhile. It is what, in the end, allows us to grow old and die with dignity.

This section will explore several areas where the Cool Positive energy of Accomplishment expresses itself. The chapter on control is, paradoxically, about letting go of control, of letting the wisdom of the situation express itself. Generosity is the classic expression of the accomplished spirit, when the self is open and unguarded and can freely share with others. From a sense of Accomplishment comes gratitude, a thankfulness to be here, alive with everyone. And last, power expresses Accomplishment not when it imposes from without but when it abides within, in the integrity of a mature, developed character.

I started this book by pointing out that the workplace is one area of our life where we are not fully in control. In other areas of our life we are quite independent. We rent or own our own home, we are free to think and say what we want, to influence the course of political and community life, to travel freely, to worship without constraint, and to enjoy all the fruits of modern civilization. But in the workplace, we are hostage to a variety of forces—our immediate superiors, company

policy, government regulation, union rules, the caprice of the marketplace. That is one reason why so many people are willing to sacrifice the security of a regular paycheck to strike out on their own. That feeling of independence, of being in charge of your own destiny, is worth a great deal. It certainly was to me.

But in a spiritual sense, control of any kind is an illusion. We are never fully in control of anything—not our health or our possessions, not the weather, not our spouse or our children, not our job, not our community, not our country or other nations. (The one exception, as I have said so often in this book, is our inner life.) All our technological miracles have obscured just how unpredictable and out-of-control human life still is. The first lesson of Buddhist teaching is the principle of

The wind moves the kite, but you hold the string. You, the wind, and the kite are one.

impermanence: Nothing lasts, nothing can be counted on, everything changes. That is another way of saying that we can't control anything in our world, at least not for long. Everything is continually slipping through our grasp.

When we feel in control—in other words, when things are going as we want them to—we feel good. We feel calm, relaxed, and at ease. In the terminology of the Energy Wheel, we are in the realm of Cool Positive. But beneath the surface of that feeling lies some anxiety. Suppose something unexpected happens. Suppose this good situation ends. Suppose the boss changes his mind. Suppose the big client is wooed away by a competitor. Suppose the floods rise and wash out the warehouse. Suppose this, suppose that. That is why we cling to our success—to hang on to our good fortune, so that it will not turn on us and slip away.

Many of the management activities in the workplace—the meetings, memos, directives, and team building—are all efforts to get control of what is inherently an unpredictable situation. Teamwork itself—a popular buzzword these days—is more complicated than it appears. A team is not just a bunch of people in a room. Inspiring a sense of shared vision, cooperation, and trust is difficult to bring off, even for the most talented manager. The Saturn division of General Motors, long touted as a model of team-based management, was recently reported to be having second thoughts. Many of the workers wanted to scrap the team approach and go back to the old six-hundred-page United Auto Workers contract. I'm sure that bulky contract seemed more solid and predictable than the difficult and ephemeral task of sustaining real teamwork.

In business, as in life, there are no easy answers. I often say in my talks that if business were a sure thing, anyone could be good at it. Being able to manage uncertainty is what separates those who prosper in business from those who do not. And managing uncertainty is a skill as valuable in the spiritual world as it is in business. It is one thing to confront uncertainty and doubt in a meditation retreat, where the outer environment is calm and controlled, but quite another to have to manage it when chaos reigns and the stakes are high.

You may have noticed that I put the title of this chapter in quotation marks—"Control." This chapter will explore a different way to be in "control" called Controlling by Paying Attention.

Right away that seems like a contradiction in terms. How can we control something or someone just by paying attention? Isn't paying attention too passive, the opposite of control? How can that be enough? Indeed, Controlling by Paying Attention is something of a paradox. It actually means giving up control, allowing things to happen, letting the unpredictability of the situation surface and play itself out, while we remain actively engaged in the drama, not just as a spectator but as a participant.

This is not what we usually mean when we say "control," but this capability still deserves to be called control in the wider sense of mastery, of having a rooted inner confidence that the situation will prosper. Think of how you "control" a kite. The wind moves the kite, but you hold the string. You don't let go of the kite, but you don't hold it close to your chest either. You let it soar. Without you, the kite can't fly. But you don't tell it where to go. You, the wind, and the kite are one. Controlling by Paying Attention means throwing yourself all the way into the situation and trusting yourself and others enough to let the wind do most of the work. Without some wisdom in our efforts to exercise control, we end up like so many managers and bosses in the workplace, resorting to rank and status to get our way with others.

Penelope, a middle manager at a large electronics manufacturing firm, had a boss who had a habit of throwing tantrums, of being vindictive and petty at management meetings. Penelope was quick to say that her boss was capable and generally well regarded, except for this unfortunate tendency, which most of his staff tolerated as unavoidable.

Once, after a particularly ugly meeting, Penelope decided she had had enough. She marched into her boss's office, sat down, and said, "Ralph, the way you acted in that meeting was unacceptable. You know none of us had anything to do with missing that deadline. It was ridiculous for you to carry on like that. Why did you do it?"

Ralph hung his head and didn't say anything for a long time. Finally he looked up at Penelope and said, "You're right. I'm sorry. I'll apologize to everyone tomorrow morning."

From that time on, Penelope noticed a change in Ralph. He didn't entirely stop his moody behavior, but she could tell he was trying to contain it. He was not a bad person, not even a bad boss. He had just succumbed to the seduction of power, which surrounded him like a plastic bubble and cut him off from others' feelings.

Ralph's actions are by no means unusual. If you are a manager, you may have found yourself occasionally behaving a bit like Ralph. And if you are someone who reports to a manager, you may have had an experience similar to Penelope's. People like Ralph do not behave the way they do because they want to hurt others. They too are responding to the stress of not having things under control. They just do not know another way.

If your job gives you a lot of conventional control, if you are a boss, or an owner, or a senior manager like Ralph, then this chapter may offer a different way to express your power and your success in a way that includes the truth of change, uncertainty, and impermanence. And if your rank or status on the job is not that high, Controlling by Paying Attention can still work for you. In the example of Ralph and Penelope, who, at that moment, was the real "boss"? Who was in control? It was Penelope, who was able to express the truth of the situation, regardless of whose title was on the door.

INTERDEPENDENCE AND SIMULTANEITY

Controlling by Paying Attention is based on two spiritual principles: Interdependence and Simultaneity.

Interdependence means that although we all seem to be separate, distinct people, we are deeply connected to others. Through our essential humanity, the universality of our basic wants and needs, and our desire to love and be loved, we share a common fate and destiny with everyone. We will explore Interdependence in greater detail in chapter 17, "Gratitude."

There are many Buddhist stories that illustrate this principle. A woman whose son had recently died came to the Buddha with her dead son in her arms and pleaded with him for medicine to restore his life. "Bring me a handful of mustard seed," the Buddha replied, "from a house where no one has ever been ill, or died, and I will help you." The woman did as she was told and traveled from door to door, asking whether anyone within was free from the experience of sickness and death. "No," one person after another told her, "someone recently died here too. We too have lost a child."

In the course of her journey the woman realized that her personal tragedy was nothing other than the human condition shared by everyone. "How selfish I am in my grief!" the woman realized as she sat by the roadside contemplating her condition. "Death is a fate shared by everyone!" She realized that in her grief she was not alone. She was connected with everyone, and everyone with her. That is how the Buddha helped her.

The principle of Simultaneity is an outcome of this connection. It means that when a thought or feeling occurs to us, it is probably occurring to someone else at the same time. That is what the woman with the dead child realized in the story. There is a saying in the Chinese Buddhist tradition that illustrates this point: "When Joe drinks whiskey, Pete becomes tipsy." Human beings are much more the same than they are different. And aside from that shared fate, we are also social animals, who have evolved over millennia to cooperate, to join forces, to share and interact. Our thoughts and feelings, our inspirations and insights, are not our unique possession but flow naturally from one person to another. If I have an inspiration or a good idea, chances are someone, somewhere, is thinking along the same lines. If I smile, my neighbor is happier. If I frown, my colleague begins to worry. In the workplace, this natural affinity of one person to another is often masked by the organization, hierarchy, and culture of competition. Even so, Simultaneity can be a resource, as we shall shortly see.

WHAT IS ATTENTION?

Attention is the core skill of a spiritual life. Every spiritual practice, to one degree or another, requires it. Attention means to notice what is really happening, as opposed to what we imagine is happening. For example, when we pay attention to our breathing in meditation, we are tuning in to a much more fundamental reality than the inner and outer dialogues that usually absorb most of our waking hours. The searchlight of the mind's attention can be pointed anywhere, but how often is it consciously pointed where we wish it to be? That difference is one boundary line between conventional life and spiritual life.

One of my favorite stories concerns the sixteenth-century Japanese Buddhist master Ikkyu, who was the abbot of a famous Buddhist temple. One day, a wealthy patron paid him a visit and asked Ikkyu if he would create a calligraphy scroll for him. Obligingly, Ikkyu took up paper and brush and rapidly wrote the single Chinese character for attention.

This was not quite what the patron had in mind. "Perhaps the Master will write something more?" he politely inquired.

Without a word, Ikkyu picked up the brush and wrote the same character again: "Attention!"

The patron was becoming annoyed. He was hoping to have an inspirational poem he could hang in the central alcove of his mansion to impress his visitors. "Surely the Master is not finished with his poem."

Equally annoyed, Ikkyu picked up the brush and in rapid succession wrote three times, "Attention! Attention! Attention!"

In a spiritual sense, attention is more than ordinary watching and listening, different from the concentration needed to do a crossword puzzle or thread a needle. Spiritual attention includes being attentive to what is *not* evident to your eyes and ears, being open to what has not yet been said, being aware of the edges of a situation. It works best when our focus is rather soft, like the quality of light at dusk. In twilight, we cannot see the sharp edges of things so clearly, but the *possibility* of what things might be, including what we ourselves can contribute to the situation, is stronger. That is why dusk is a time of magic and poetry, when the boundary between the inner and the outer world becomes soft. What is that rustling in the bushes? Is it a quail, or is it a bear? We can't see, so our imagination includes both possibilities.

This is why martial arts students are taught to cultivate a "soft gaze," in which they do not look directly at their opponent but at the space surrounding him. This seems odd when you first try it, but in fact it is the only way to see the whole picture. At the same time, just because this kind of attention is "soft" does not mean it is passive or disengaged. On the contrary, it is energized and focused.

Suppose you have arranged to meet your spouse or partner in the lobby of a downtown hotel but forgot to specify which entrance. You can't get in touch, so all you can do is go to the hotel and position yourself in a central location where you can see all the entrances and revolving doors.

Perhaps it is a special occasion, such as an anniversary dinner. So whether or not you meet matters a great deal. You know exactly what you are there to do and what you want to accomplish. But in order to have the best chance of spotting your loved one, you can't just stare fixedly at one door. You have to soften your gaze, moving your glance from door to door, to make sure you don't miss your mark. You have to open yourself up to multiple possibilities.

LETTING GO OF CONTROL

How can this approach be applied in the workplace?

William was a vice president of operations in a chain of women's apparel boutiques. His team was responsible for the day-to-day management of forty stores nationwide. Because of the firm's rapid growth, William's whole department lived under a daily cloud of impending crisis. There was always some kind of emergency at one of the stores, whether it was a shipment delay, a broken water main, a store manager's sudden resignation, or a street crew cutting the store's computer link to the home office.

William had attained his position because he was a problem solver who knew how to get things done. The most important part of his day was the morning staff meeting, at which he and his staff reviewed and prioritized the tasks for the day. These meetings were famous for their rapid pace and near-military terseness. The format was always the same. A staff member would report a problem; after brief discussion, William would ratify the team's solution or propose one of his own. He would assign responsibility for the task and move on.

The firm's annual performance review included comments from subordinates. William had just had his review at the time I met him, and while his overall performance score was high, his subordinates criticized his management style, using such phrases as "doesn't listen," "imperious," "overly critical," "impatient with suggestions."

For several years, I had had a job similar to William's and had received some of the same criticisms. My temperament is quick and impatient, and verbally dominating. If I want to, I can usually get my way, but needless to say that mode is not the best for fostering teamwork. Over time, I tried to apply what I had learned from my Buddhist training and came up with the following steps:

1. When I was in a meeting or in conversation with an individual, whenever a good response or a solution came up, whether it was my own or someone else's, rather than immediately acting or speaking I instead visualized that response going "into the room," like a puff of smoke, and just let it stay there for a while.

2. If I felt the conversation drifting or becoming unproductive, rather than immediately acting to refocus it, I let it go. Sometimes I found it helpful to actually verbalize this intention: "Let it go, let it go." Other times I would invoke a self-mantra: "Waiting, waiting, waiting . . ."

3. If I felt an uncontrollable urge to speak, I tried to speak neutrally and say as little as possible. (This was hard!)

4. I watched and paid attention to whatever happened next.

Sometimes I found that it helped to "throw" my impatience into a physical object in the room, such as a vase of flowers or a piece of furniture. This worked better than biting my tongue! It gave my impatience a place to rest and gave me a safe place to focus my attention.

What I found is that often the direction in which I wanted to move the conversation occurred whether I intervened in it or not. Because the energy of the solution was already in the room, it found a way to express itself. What's more, because I was not imposing my will as I used to do, the group had more of a sense that decisions were being arrived at by the group, not just me.

I also found the practice quite difficult, as did William, when he decided to try it. For impatient people like William and me, the experience of letting the situation take its own course can be excruciating. But whenever I could manage to do so, I felt a sense of satisfaction. Over time, my team began to pull together more and became less dependent on me.

At first, William's experience wasn't quite as positive as mine had been. For him, the main effect of his effort to practice Controlling by Paying Attention was that everything took longer. Often, when the time for his daily staff meeting was up, no one had come up with the solution he favored and he still had to impose it.

"What kinds of solutions did come up?"

"They weren't bad," William admitted. "But they usually weren't as good as mine. Most of those people just don't have my experience in how to solve these problems."

"Were they ever better than yours?" I asked.

"Sometimes," William admitted.

I asked him if he had tried "throwing" his solution into a physical object. William admitted that he found that idea bizarre and hadn't really felt comfortable trying it.

"Well, how about this," I said. "Whenever it occurs to you to say something, say it silently to yourself. See if the other people in the room can hear what you are saying."

William thought this was nearly as strange as "throwing" his thoughts into a vase of flowers, but he agreed to try it.

The next week, his report was more encouraging. Strangely enough, when he silently "shouted" at the group, there did seem, sometimes, to be a shift in the group's direction toward the solution he favored.

Controlling by Paying Attention is a method that depends on faith in our fellow human beings to be at their best, to know what you know, to think what you think. Ultimately, this is not control as much as it is respect. William was already the boss in the situation. Everybody looked to him as the final decision maker. In other words, everyone was already paying attention to him! He just needed to pay more attention to them.

Deborah Tannen explored some of this ground in her bestselling book *You Just Don't Understand*. There she describes two different communication styles, one that sees conversation as a kind of competition and another that sees it more as collaboration. One feature of the competitive style of conversation is that the person will pay close attention to the tiny gaps in the conversation where he can interject or, in some cases, interrupt. A person using the collaborative style is more interested in drawing the other person out, in listening attentively.

Although these two styles are different, both require close attention. The competitive talker is watching for a place to interject, while the collaborative person pays receptive attention to the other person's words. William's style was more competitive, and that is why I suggested he try a more collaborative approach. For someone whose style is more collaborative to begin with, and whose main difficulty is getting a word in edgewise, some combination of the two may be the answer. Both methods subtly change the dynamic of the give-and-take in conversation. The collaborative style is closer in spirit to Controlling by Paying Attention, but some of the techniques we have mentioned, such as "shouting" silently, make use of the competitive style's energy. In either style, it is the attention itself that counts. Paying attention is a powerful energy. It only seems private and invisible to the person doing it. To others, it is a tangible force, whether they are consciously aware of it or not.

WAITING FOR THE RIGHT MOMENT

Controlling by Paying Attention is not only a communication style. It reflects an attitude of generosity and patience, and can be a way of teaching, of making a suggestion, and of giving feedback.

One of the hardest parts of being a manager is having to give criticism to your subordinates. Sometimes no matter what you do, the criticism is poorly received. No one likes to be criticized. Any criticism, even if skillfully given, may lead to resentment by the employee. After a while, many managers avoid giving criticism at all, although that isn't a good solution either.

There is a middle ground between withholding criticism and giving it, and that is to pay close attention to the situation without saying anything until the right moment. If someone working for you has a problem, closely observing that person is a far cry from not doing anything about it. The attention itself becomes a force for change, as well as a way to catch the best moment to intervene.

I first learned this by watching how Suzuki Roshi taught us. He didn't give much direct instruction and rarely criticized. Instead, he would observe someone for weeks without saying anything, until an opportune moment arose. Then he would say what he wanted to say. Because the moment was right, his words went right to the heart.

One summer at the monastery, it was my job to clean his cabin. Although we had ordinary mops, I wanted to clean things Japanese style, so I wiped his wood floor down every morning with a damp towel. He was usually nearby when I did this, sometimes in the cabin attending to other work, or sometimes just outside it, in his garden. I polished the floor with great diligence, and for more than two weeks he never said anything.

One morning, he came over and, without a word, took the towel from me, folded it in a long, narrow rectangle, got down on his hands and knees, and demonstrated drawing the towel in long, broad strokes up and down the floor. It was a much more efficient way to do the job. He could have shown me on the first day, but I think he wanted me to struggle on my own first. Though I wasn't aware of it, he had been observing me every day. That was what made his intervention so effective for me. It was not just that he showed me a different method for doing the task. He also demonstrated his concern for me. That was far more important than the towel.

There is a story about the poet-monk Ryokan, who lived in eighteenth-century Japan, that illustrates the same point. The dissolute son of a prominent merchant in Ryokan's village had gotten into trouble and was the disgrace of the family. As a last resort, the merchant invited Ryokan to spend a few weeks in his home as his guest, in the hopes that Ryokan could do something to help the young man turn his life around.

Day after day went by, and to the merchant's dismay Ryokan appeared to do nothing at all. He hardly even spoke to the boy. Several times the merchant took Ryokan aside and implored him to say something to his son. Ryokan smiled and nodded, but more time passed and still he said nothing. Finally, on the day of Ryokan's departure, as he was standing in the vestibule putting on his traveling garments, the dissolute son came to the doorway and as his social duty bent down to tie the honored guest's straw sandals.

Suddenly, without knowing why, the young man looked up into Ryokan's face and saw a single tear glistening on Ryokan's cheek. The son realized that the tear was for him. After that, so the story goes, the son was a changed man. Looking up into Ryokan's face had transformed him. The merchant was overjoyed and sent Ryokan a letter of thanks with an expensive gift enclosed. "I don't know what you did," the merchant wrote, "but my son is a new person."

Ryokan returned the gift with a short note. "Thank you for your gift, which I cannot accept. I did nothing to change your son. Everything that has happened he accomplished himself."

Ryokan was not being modest, just truthful. We can imagine how the son must have felt during the two-week visit. He was no fool. He knew that this was another of his father's schemes to make him shape up. Every day he waited for the priest to scold him, to tell him he was no good the way his father did. But Ryokan said nothing. He just observed the young man closely, without criticizing or commenting. He trusted in the youth's good nature, his own emerging maturity.

Ryokan understood that if you watch closely enough, and trust enough, transformation unfolds in its own fashion. Would that modern workplaces were patient enough, and respectful enough, to allow us to grow in that way. Some workplaces are. Some managers instinctively understand these principles and enact them every day in their interactions with others.

Most people want to excel and do well. If we don't try to control them but let them soar like the kite on the end of a string, who knows what will happen?

Practices for "Control"

- When you feel compelled to say something in a meeting or a conversation, wait. See what happens if you simply watch and listen.

- When you feel you must criticize someone, first spend more time simply observing that person. Wait for an opportune moment.

- Can you find instances of Simultaneity and Interdependence in your work? Do you find echoes of your own thoughts and ideas in others' contributions? Can you build on these connections in a way that fosters teamwork and cooperation rather than competition?

- If you are a manager, can you use these principles to provide leadership and direction without "pulling rank"?

How do we feel when we are generous? Confident, relaxed, open, at ease—exactly how we have described the Cool Positive region of the Energy Wheel. Generosity is a tangible expression of the self's openness, of our willingness to feel other people's sorrow and desire other people's happiness. Generosity is also what keeps spiritual life from becoming too inward, too self-absorbed. Through the spirit of generosity we directly experience our connection with others. Peo-

ple often associate Buddhism with meditation, but in the sixfold classification of Buddhist spiritual virtues, meditation is fifth. Generosity is first.

Generosity is not a spiritual add-on; it is fundamental. That is why there are so many areas of our life—family, church, community, and philanthropy—where we give of ourselves unconditionally, without thought of reward. We don't charge our children for the costs of bringing them up. We don't send our friend a bill after we have helped him move. We don't charge for our time at the hospital where we volunteer. Before there were jobs, before there were occupations, before there was money, before there were even villages or towns, people practiced generosity. It is something we all instinctively know how to do.

To be present is the most fundamental generosity of all. When there is nothing else to do, when we are in a situation that seems hopelessly blocked, there is still one thing we can do: We can be there.

Of course, people don't abandon generosity when they come to work. But the energy of the workplace is not like that of the church or the family. We are paid for what we do—that's what makes a job a job. And naturally we expect to be paid as much as possible. When is the last time you heard of anyone going into his or her boss's office to ask for a *reduction* in pay? As a last resort, union members may volunteer to take a pay cut to save their jobs, but, as a rule, in the job market, everyone's skills have a price tag.

In the world of work for pay, we compete with others for rewards, we negotiate for the best deal, and we measure our value to our employer with the universal yardstick of all commerce—money. In the realm of generosity, all those considerations are set aside. The value of what we do does not need to be measured. It is already there. We do not need to be rewarded. By definition, a generous act seeks no reward.

All of us migrate frequently between these two worlds. In the middle of our workday we invite our good friend to lunch to commiserate with her about her recent divorce. While helping our child with her homework, the phone rings and it is the boss with an urgent request. It is not hard to alternate from one mode to the other, but it is more difficult to bring them together.

In the Buddhist center where I spent many years as a teacher, we started several small businesses to support ourselves—a restaurant, a bakery, a bookstore, and a clothing store. We didn't describe these enterprises as businesses. Rather, we thought of them as an extension of our spiritual life. We called them "practice places." In order to support the center, people were paid only about half the market value for their work. The jobs of waiter, baker, and sewer were thought of as opportunities to deepen spiritual practice in the company of like-minded fellows.

On the surface, this seemed like a wonderful fusion of the spiritual and the commercial, but underneath, there were tensions. At one point, I wrote a memo to my colleagues in the center's leadership suggesting that we pay everyone the full market value for their work, and let each person voluntarily give back a portion as a tangible (and tax-deductible) donation. That way, the contribution of each worker to the center, and of the center to each worker, could be kept separate.

This suggestion was not well received. At that time in our development, we imagined that money wasn't important, that to differentiate between work and donation would be confusing rather than clarifying. Nevertheless, over time, people began to feel exploited. Eventually, the businesses evolved into more conventional, independently managed enterprises.

GENEROSITY AT WORK

The story of the center's businesses demonstrates that even with the best of intentions it is not so easy to join the spiritual with the commercial. I think one of the flaws in our effort was that we were trying to dictate from above how everyone's generosity was supposed to function. That didn't work. For generosity to be authentic, it has to flow freely from the heart—not as a thought or idea but as a feeling.

My observation is that people try to be generous to their workplace colleagues whenever they can. As I have already said, generosity is intrinsic to who we are. But because the workplace operates according to its own logic and rules, generosity doesn't always function there the way it does in our personal life. It can sometimes be misinterpreted or go awry. At other times, as in the following story, it works even though its recipients aren't quite sure what is happening.

JUST BE KIND

A well-known movie actor, let's call him Curtis, told this story about workplace generosity. A movie set, he explained, is like a medieval court. The director is the king. The actors, particularly the stars, are the nobles and courtiers; they often have their own power bases and may contend with the king. All the technicians and workers are the servants, who are treated in a businesslike manner as they are told what to do but are given no real status.

Curtis, a practicing Buddhist, decided that his spiritual practice required treating everyone as an equal, with kindness and respect, regardless of his or her perceived status in the movie world. He didn't do it to make a splash, or to criticize, or to advertise his spiritual credentials. He just felt better doing it that way.

He was not prepared for the reaction his behavior elicited. People often approached him with puzzled looks on their faces and asked, "Curtis, what are you doing? Is this some spiritual thing? Why are you being so nice to people?"

"It's a cold business," Curtis explained to me. "Even the actors don't get a lot of respect. The director will come up to you and pat the side of your neck and say, 'Curtis, you gotta work out more. Look at all these wrinkles. Can't we put a scarf around this or something?'" Curtis gave a perfect imitation of a tough-talking Hollywood director. "Just to be nice to people, just to treat them as equals, as ordinary human beings, is radical. It shakes things up on a deep level."

I was interested to know if there were any untoward consequences of Curtis's change of attitude. But when I asked him about it, he just laughed. "It's Hollywood," he said, shrugging, "and I'm an actor. Everybody knows actors are strange. They figured this was just my personal weirdness."

"And did you keep it up?" I asked.

"I did," Curtis said. "And word began to get around. I think it helped my career. It's a competitive business, and being known as supportive and easy to work with can be a tie-breaker in close calls."

In Curtis's workplace and probably in many others, just being kind came across as weird. This is certainly a sobering thought. It makes one wonder what kind of world we have created in our work.

In my workshops, we often enter into a free-ranging discussion about what kinds of generosity work well in the workplace. Here are some of them.

RIGHT SPEECH

Speech is an integral and necessary part of most jobs. Some jobs—most management positions, for example—are primarily concerned with writing and talking. It is easy to fall into a pattern of "efficient" speech—quick, brusque, lacking in courtesy and finesse. After all, as a hard-driving businessperson might say, "We are not at a dinner party, we're on the job!" But speech, both written and spoken, can also be one of the best ways to practice generosity. Efficiency and generosity need not be mutually exclusive.

Buddhism includes a teaching called Right Speech. Traditionally, Right Speech means speech that is kind, inoffensive, honest, and respectful. The pressures of a busy workplace sometimes make it difficult to practice Right Speech with a Buddhist monk's thoroughness, but we can all make efforts in this direction. In its broadest sense, Right Speech is *conscious* speech: We pay attention to what we are saying and how we are saying it. Sometimes what conveys generosity in speech is a matter of the tone, pacing, facial expressions, and body language as much as our actual words.

Even criticism can be delivered in such a way that it conveys generosity. For example, consider the difference between these two approaches:

"Jeffrey, your performance is not up to snuff. You're going to have to shape up. And soon!"

"Jeffrey, I'm concerned about your performance. It really isn't measuring up to the standard I expected. I know you're making an effort, and I'd like to discuss what you need to do to correct the situation."

Both statements deliver the message, but the second message includes some sense of recognition, participation, and respect. For example, a person's effort is always worth mentioning, even if it falls short of what is required. Good managers often have an instinctive sense of how to phrase their statements in a way that makes people feel honored for who they are. One of the best managers I ever knew was able to accomplish this without saying anything at all. Just the way that he listened told the whole story, so much so that people outside of his department often consulted with him unofficially about their problems. More than once when I was going home at night I would see people outside his office, none of whom worked directly for him, waiting for a chance to have a few minutes with him.

"I like talking with Ernie about things" was how one person explained it to me. "He makes me feel good about myself."

Right Speech needn't always be soft and gentle. Sometimes an expression of frustration, irritation, or even anger can function as Right Speech if it is done in the right spirit. It all depends, ultimately, on the intention behind our words and the skill and conscious attention with which they are crafted.

GENTLE TRUTH

Another aspect of Right Speech is honesty. The truth itself can be a gift, if it is given in the right spirit. I say "Gentle Truth" because the truth can also be hurtful. We don't want to just walk up to one of our coworkers and blurt out, "You know, you have bad breath. No one can stand to be close to you." We also need to be careful to distinguish between *our* truth, which may be just our opinion, and *the* truth, in which everyone can share.

In the previous chapter, Penelope's confronting Ralph about his surliness in meetings could be an example of Gentle Truth. If Penelope's intention was to hurt Ralph, or get back at him, then her comments would not qualify as generosity. But Ralph's response— "You're right. I'm sorry. I'll apologize to everyone tomorrow morning"—proves that there was more to Penelope's criticism than her words. Because her intention was to help Ralph, not to hurt him, the truth she offered him functioned as a gift, not just for Ralph but for Penelope herself and everyone on Ralph's team.

I am reminded of an incident that involved Suzuki Roshi during his days as a temple priest in Japan. One day he was outside his temple with another priest when a workman called down to them from the roof, where he was making repairs. "There you go, a couple of lazy priests who don't work for a living. What good are you to anyone?" Suzuki looked up at the roofer without saying anything for a while. At last, he called out to the roofer, "That temple next door has a beautiful roof."

Now, besides the fact that the temple next door was well known throughout the district for its beautiful tile roof, what relevance did this comment have to the worker's rude remark? None at all, unless we understood Suzuki Roshi's words as an offering of truth. If we wanted to take that thought further, we could say that Suzuki Roshi was introducing into the conversation something that he and the roofer could agree on, regardless of the roofer's opinion of priests or of him.

PRESENCE

Have you ever noticed how the word *present* can be used as an adjective, a noun, or a verb? To be present means to be there. A present is a gift. And "to present" means to offer. When senators or congresspeople don't wish to go on record as either for or against, how do they vote? "Present!"

To be present is the most fundamental generosity of all. When there is nothing else to do, when we are in a situation that seems hopelessly blocked, there is still one thing we can do: We can be there. When a person is in pain, or is suffering, or is intensely sad, or is ill, instead of feeling helpless or letting our head swim with a thousand unhelpful solutions, we can just be present. Presence is also the secret behind the topic of the previous chapter, Controlling by Paying Attention. Remember the story of Ryokan and the wayward youth, or William and his team of troubleshooters? In both cases, it was the power of presence that won the day.

In my office, I function as both the president and chief programmer, and there is never enough of me to go around. Everyone wants a chunk of my time for this or that. In order to protect my own responsibilities and be sure that at the end of the day I have accomplished something, my tendency is to to cut the conversation short and give a little less of myself than my employees would like. In a previous job, I had one colleague who used to signal his impatience with the phrase "Moving right along!" But when you are in a position like mine, just to be there is useful. To be present is generous—even, in an indirect way, productive. I have to keep reminding myself of that.

To be truly present, it is not enough to drop ourselves into a chair like a sack of potatoes. Being present in a generous sense means to be fully present, with all our faculties, attention, and care. Try it the next time you find yourself edging out of the room. What would your presence for ten or fifteen seconds more cost you? And what might you and the people who are with you gain?

Once when I was hospitalized for some surgery, a local clergyman was visiting me. As we chatted, the stout middle-aged woman who cleaned my room every day came in to sweep the floor and empty the trash cans. When she left, the clergyman gestured toward the doorway and said, "She's the healer."

I didn't quite understand what he meant at first. But later, when I thought about it more, I realized that every time that woman came into my room, I felt better. Her quiet, unobtrusive presence as she went about her work indeed had a caring, healing quality. In the pecking order of hospital employees, she was undoubtedly at the bottom, but I would guess that in her own community, people treated her with admiration and respect. She had the power to change the whole feeling in the room just by being there. We don't learn how to do that in college or business school. That ability comes from faith, from character, from God.

SEEING AND HEARING WITH THE HEART

To see people fully is different from just looking at them. To hear people deeply is not the same as simply registering what they are saying. The organ that sees in generosity is not just the eye. The organ that hears in generosity is not just the ear; it is the heart. To See and Hear with the Heart means to offer yourself forward, to act with generosity in full attention. This is not a passive action. It is a conscious act of will, of intention.

"To Hear with the Heart" is not a metaphorical expression. We actually do it with the heart, from our chest, in the center of our body. We have spoken of this practice before, in chapter 13, when we introduced the Friend in the Heart meditation. This is an extension of that practice toward other people.

Suppose Cathy, your subordinate, pokes her head into your office and says, "I'm not feeling well. I think I'll go home early." If you glance up briefly from your work and say, "All right, I hope you feel better tomorrow," that is hearing with the ear. If, instead, you fully absorb the message, if you open up your heart not just to what Cathy is saying but also to what she is feeling and empathize with her fully, then you are hearing not just with the ear but with the heart. Your heart may encompass a history of knowledge about Cathy, such as the fact that she is suffering from a chronic illness that at some point may require surgery, and that in addition to not feeling well Cathy is uneasy, even frightened, about that prospect.

You may say, "I would like to be able to be that caring and empathetic about everyone I work with, and I do the best I can, but I can't be responsible for everyone's personal life." That is a reasonable objection, and I am not asking you to become your office's designated saint! Nevertheless, as an exercise in generosity, you might experiment with the difference between ordinary hearing and the kind of hearing I have described above. The next time you are with a good friend, or someone with whom it is natural for you to be heartfelt, see if you can sense what is different about Hearing with the Heart. What you may find is that while your mind follows the meaning of the conversation, some other part of yourself, your heart, is tuning in to the feeling behind the words. In that sense the heart is another kind of sensory organ, whose job it is to feel what others feel. And then, at work, notice the next time you are listening more mechanically—for example, when you are listening to a boring presentation—and see if you can sense what is different and what is missing. In that situation, the heart as an organ of feeling is not activated. It is asleep.

You are not obligated to perform these subtle acts of generosity at any particular time, or with any special frequency. There is no shame if you feel you cannot do it very often. But sometimes, when you think you can, give it a try. That shift of energy from the eye and ear to the heart may seem like a private, invisible matter. But the other person can feel and appreciate it, whether he or she is conscious of it or not.

There is no need to say anything special or unusual to note your shift of energy. In the example I mentioned earlier, perhaps all that would be different would be a pause before you said to Cathy, "All right." In that short pause, a lot can happen, a lot of energy can move. If you add, "I'm sorry you are continuing to have this problem. I am concerned for you," that is good too. But even though you say you're concerned, if you don't really feel it, then the generosity doesn't really flow. If you feel the sincerity of your energy in your heart, then Cathy will feel it too.

GENEROSITY TO AN ADVERSARY

In the workplace there can be people who dislike you, who are out to get you, who would rather see you fail. There is nothing special about generosity to an adversary, it is just harder. We are angry with the adversary. We don't want to help her, we want to protect ourselves from her, or even do her harm. Our mind is filled with cutting remarks, accusations, and lists of faults and failings.

Anna worked in an advertising firm. She was one of the two best account managers in the firm, the other being Cecile. It seemed as though their boss, the senior manager, might be moving to another division, opening up a promotion path for either Anna or Cecile. Their boss's recommendation to top management would count for a lot.

One day Anna needed to consult with Cecile about something. When she went down the hall to Cecile's office she noticed that the door was half open. Gently pushing on the door, she poked her head in and spoke Cecile's name.

Cecile's response was to berate her for not knocking. "How can you come barging in here like that?" she snapped at Anna. "That's the whole problem with you. You just don't have any respect for other people!"

This outburst caught Anna off guard. She quickly apologized and left. Later that day she heard that Cecile had gone directly to their boss and complained about Anna's attitude problem. A couple of weeks later, the new promotion was announced. Cecile had gotten the job.

Does it seem as though Anna was blindsided by an unscrupulous colleague? Does her predicament resonate with similar experiences in your own work life? Given this unsavory situation, how might Anna practice generosity toward her adversary, Cecile?

It's not easy to be generous in such circumstances. But what is the alternative? Does Anna continue to harbor a grudge against Cecile for the rest of her tenure there? (Remember, Cecile is now Anna's boss!) Does Anna quit in frustration? (In real life this is what Anna actually did!) Or does Anna find a way to rise above the situation, unjust though it may have been, and treat Cecile with the fairness and dignity that Cecile denied her?

If you are in a situation like this, you have to decide for yourself what you are comfortable doing. If you are willing to try being generous toward your adversary, here are some suggestions that might help.

First, you can offer your adversary (and yourself) the gift of trying not to make things any worse. In the case of Anna, that means containing her anger and relating to Cecile in a professional manner. This does not mean caving in to Cecile. It means honoring what is right and admirable in yourself. Insofar as this approach prevents Cecile from continuing her ill will toward Anna, this outcome actually helps both of them.

Next, you can practice "standing sideways." In the days of duels with pistols, the antagonists stood sideways as they raised and aimed their pistols to present as little a target as possible. When you contribute to your adversary's ability to hurt you by acting in ways that present a broad target, you are not only hurting yourself but also allowing your adversary to bring out the worst in herself. No adversary is wholly bad. There are redeeming qualities in everyone. One way to bring them out is to model them for your adversary. Act your best, and your adversaries will have a harder time acting their worst.

And as a final suggestion, practice Seeing and Hearing with the Heart, taking extra care to remain in the heart even when all your alarm bells tell you that you are being disrespected, attacked, or challenged. In actual conversation, this often boils down to a kind of openhearted silence or minimal response, not taking the bait. This benefits you, and it serves as a gift to your adversary.

That is the magic of generosity. When it is real, giving of ourselves freely is the most fundamental way to help ourselves, whereas behavior that is selfish and narrow-minded, even if it seems to be to our benefit, tends to diminish us in the long run. Generosity doesn't always make sense rationally, but it makes sense spiritually. That is because in the spiritual realm, people are not separate, they are connected—by temperament, by nature, and by shared fate.

Young children give of themselves this way because they have not unlearned the impulse and lost their innocence. That is why it is a joy to be around them, because their enthusiasm to share their world with us is beautiful. We cannot be innocent children at work. But we can protect ourselves and at the same time be open to opportunities to give.

BE STRATEGIC

In a folktale of ancient India, a village was being terrorized by a cobra whose aggressive attacks had already resulted in the deaths of several people. They tried to capture the cobra but he was too quick for them, and in desperation the villagers called in a holy man. The holy man found the cobra's den and scolded the cobra. "You must not injure people anymore. That is against the law of the gods."

The cobra was contrite and promised he would not harm anyone. The next time the villagers found the cobra, they attacked it with sticks and stones and beat the cobra nearly to death. The cobra crawled away to where the holy man sat and complained. "Look at me!" the cobra said. "Because of your advice I am nearly dead. How can that be the law of the gods?"

"I said you were not to bite people anymore," the holy man said. "I never said you couldn't hiss."

Generosity in the workplace does not mean giving up all sense and strategy about how to survive and protect ourselves on the job.

But it does mean that when a choice presents itself—when we have an opportunity to open our heart and let generosity flow from it rather than to close it up and armor ourselves—we can choose the path of the heart.

Sometimes we are surprised and delighted at the outcome. And even if the outcome is not good, don't give up. To do the hard thing, to be generous when it seems to be foolish to do so, may make others feel good. And even if it doesn't, you will feel good and will be more likely to try again and again, until the day when the effort bears fruit and something bright opens.

I don't know what would have happened if Anna had stayed on her job. I don't know whether Cecile got the job because of her machinations and complaints. By quitting, Anna may have made the right decision—for her. But I do know, because I myself have been there, that for Anna to try to fight fire with fire, to become as ruthless and calculating as she imagined Cecile to be, doesn't work at all.

Trust the heart, use the heart, but take good care of the heart. Be practical, be savvy, protect yourself, hiss when you have to, like the cobra in the folktale, but remember who you really are. The title on your door, the job description on your résumé, the answer you give when people ask you what you do, are not the whole of it.

Let's practice generosity whenever we can, because, in this world, it is our deepest and most reliable calling. Herb, the insurance executive whose story began this section, learned long after his career was over that what counted in the end was not the millions of dollars of insurance policies he had sold but his freely given acts of generosity that had made a lasting mark on others.

Generosity is the highest and deepest Accomplishment of all.

PRACTICES FOR GENEROSITY

- When you are listening to someone, see if you can notice the shift between hearing with the ear and Hearing with the Heart. What is that difference?

- Remember the gift of Presence. Just to be there is the most fundamental generosity of all.

- Practice kindness, particularly when you feel irritated or things are not going well. Kindness hardly ever goes wrong.

- Pay attention to what you say and how you say it. Can you practice Right Speech as conscious speech? Even a critical comment can contain some element of generosity.

- How can you give yourself and your adversary the gift of not making things worse?

The theme of this chapter is interdependence. Interdependence teaches us that we are all connected and that whatever we do has a far-reaching effect on others, beyond what we can know. The Reverend Kosho Uchiyama, a Buddhist priest of modern Japan who was also a comic strip artist, liked to draw human beings as funny-faced zucchini plants, all with their separate, individual faces but each connected by a long, winding stem to a common source. That common source is

what nourishes us all, and when our personal zucchini plant is fortunate enough to grow fat and strong, to become wealthy and powerful, it can draw strength away from all the other zucchini, as well as the root of the plant. We must remember that if our individual plant becomes too greedy, too demanding of the roots and branches, the rest of the plant will suffer and, eventually, we too will weaken.

Every person in the world is a shining jewel.

Interdependence is to some extent a synonym for spiritual life. If the word *spiritual* means anything, it means our connection to something greater than ourselves—to our community, to all life, to the cosmos, to God. That is why all of Buddhism can be summarized in that single word: *Interdependence*. The Buddha taught that when we see ourselves as separate, we suffer. But when we see ourselves as unbounded, connected and continuous with everything else that lives, even with grasses, rivers, and stones, we are liberated and full of joy.

Everything we do expresses this connection, especially the work that we do. Work is one of the main ways we express our membership in the vast network called life. We are not hermits, living in remote caves and surviving on roots and berries. We live in communities, to which each of us contributes in some fashion. Some of us are teachers, some are bankers, some are pharmacists and plumbers. We are all needed. None of us could survive alone. There is no such thing as a zucchini plant with only one zucchini. If someone were to ask me to explain in a few words the relationship between work and spirituality, I would say just this: Work is Interdependence, and Interdependence is the essence of spirit.

You may find it difficult to find anything innately spiritual in the work you do. That is not because its spirit is lacking, but because it is concealed. To the extent that we can find a spiritual practice that reveals Interdependence in the workplace—and that is the purpose of this chapter—we are not adding something new, just highlighting something that is already there.

EXPRESSING GRATITUDE

What does it mean to be grateful? Why do we say "thank you" when someone serves or helps us?

Most of the time we don't think about it that much. It is just something we all do several times a day. We thank the doorman for holding the door open for us when we enter a hotel. We thank the mailroom clerk for delivering a package to our office. We thank the doctor who gives us medicine for our illness. How many times in a day do we say those magic words *thank you* without stopping to ask "Why am I doing this? What do I really mean?"

Saying "thank you" has something to do with Interdependence and with loneliness. If we lived all alone, if there was no one to help us, if no one smiled at us, held out a hand to us, or loved us, the world would be an intolerably cruel place. Who would want to live in such a world? When we express our gratitude, we are recognizing that once again, to our surprise, the world still wants us and cares for us. The world invites us to be part of something larger than ourselves, to be a part of the whole.

When we say "thank you," we are thanking the world that, in spite of everything, love continues. We are pleased and gratified, and the smile on our face and the energy in our voice confirms it.

PUTTING GRATITUDE INTO THE ETHER

How can we bring this feeling to life in the workplace? One way is to express, in our words and actions, a sense of gratitude.

Because my firm sells software to large corporations, much of our marketing and sales activity involves calling busy executives, arranging for on-site visits to demonstrate our product, and so on. It is not unusual for us to get a phone call from a prospective client and end up spending several thousand dollars to travel across the country to demonstrate what we have to offer.

Once that has happened, we have a keen interest in closing the sale. Sometimes the client will call back and take the initiative himself. At other times, despite our repeated phone calls and voice mail messages, we will hear nothing. You might think that as a matter of courtesy, especially when we have gone to significant effort and expense to respond to the client's invitation, the client would at least let us know whether or not we had a future with him.

But that is not the standard business practice. To the typical corporation, we are a mere vendor, and the accepted etiquette regarding a vendor follows a logic like this: You are a vendor. We owe you nothing. You have a product to sell, and we might be interested. Show it to us. If we like it, we will call you back. If not, we won't.

This is not considered rudeness. It is just the way business is done in our contemporary world. You may encounter it in your own work life. I am used to it. But the Buddhist in me thinks: Something isn't quite right. There is something too linear, too logical, too cold about that kind of thinking. It is an attitude based on time and money.

The busy executive thinks, I am being paid to be effective. It is not effective, or a good use of my time, to call a vendor that I am not going to use and tell him so.

That is a valid way of thinking if you believe that the executive and the vendor are separate and different. But it is not so. The vendor and the executive work in the same industry. They know the same people. Today the executive is secure in his position, but tomorrow his situation may change. Tomorrow he may be looking for a job, and the vendor whom he saw no reason to call back may be part of a network that can help him find one. Besides, if the contracted vendor doesn't work out, the executive may have to go back and mend fences with the vendor he originally rejected.

But these are just explanations or rationalizations for why we might want to call the vendor back, even if there is nothing to say but "thanks but no thanks." The best reason for calling the vendor back is that it puts our consideration into the world, into the "ether" of Interdependence. We don't know whether anything will come of it. We are like someone putting a message into a bottle and tossing it into the ocean. We may never see our bottle again. But though the ocean is large, it is not infinite. Someone will find that bottle. Besides, if enough people start putting bottles into the ocean, the ocean will become full of bottles, and some kind of network will start to form. Some wavelike community of message-senders will take shape.

This is not mystical mumbo jumbo; it is good living and even good business. The ethos of "what's in it for me" is the way that people in the workplace rationalize rudeness and self-centered actions. That way of thinking sometimes has a direct, short-term benefit, but in the long run the most powerful arbiter of our success in the workplace is our reputation, and reputation cannot be bought or bargained for. It is who we are and the sum total of what we do. When we act from the heart, based on what we feel we ought to do rather than what is efficient, we are actually creating a deeper kind of effectiveness.

Jerry, a stockbroker, told me a story about a time early in his career when a wealthy client of his owned some corporate bonds. Because the client insisted on having personal possession of the bonds, the brokerage was not able to notify him in time that the bonds had been "called" by the company that had issued them. This meant that the bonds were worth only their face value, not the much greater value they would have had if the client had known about the call. Thus the client lost a great deal of money.

Even though Jerry's firm had no legal responsibility for what had occurred—the client insisted on keeping the bonds himself, over the firm's objections—Jerry was not comfortable with letting things stand. Technically he was in the clear, but ethically he felt responsible. He decided to pay the full amount of the client's loss out of his own account. The client, who started out being quite angry, was now gratified by this act of generosity—and the story didn't end there. For the next few weeks, when the client was at his country club, playing golf, or having dinner with his friends, what story do you think he kept telling to everyone he met? None other than the tale of his crazy stockbroker and the expired bonds! Over the next few months, Jerry gained many new clients from this unsolicited word-of-mouth advertising.

Such stories inspire us because they seem to describe responses and actions outside the workplace norm. Certainly not every stockbroker reimburses his eccentric clients out of his own pocket. Rarely does a prospect who rejects a vendor write or call. (I can testify to that!) But even if it happens one time in a hundred, or one time in a thousand, that is cause for hope. Poll takers have a phrase for a public issue that has shallow support—"a mile wide and an inch deep." I sometimes feel that the veneer of callousness and cynicism that has become the stereotype of modern business culture is just that—a veneer. Underneath that supposed layer of cynicism, another attitude is waiting to come out—gratitude.

Readers who are old enough to remember the great East Coast blackout of 1965 will recall how college students and housewives poured into the streets with flashlights to direct traffic, how people went from door to door checking on their neighbors, how in city after city—from Boston to New York to Washington, D.C.—strangers suddenly became trusted friends. Sociologists studied this event for years. How could it happen? More important, how could we elicit such a transformation without turning all the lights out again? And how could we make it last?

No one knows the answer. A Buddhist might say that we are all Buddhas waiting to happen.

BEING GRATEFUL FOR OUR SUCCESS

For people who have succeeded in their job, who are at the top of their game, who have achieved wealth, power, and influence, the practice of gratitude is particularly important. For any successful person, there is a real temptation to look at the person in the mirror and say, "Look at me! I did it! Am I not great?" Before the advent of our celebrity, media-driven culture a person of wealth was expected to behave with humility, modesty, and self-effacement—at least in public. To do otherwise was considered uncultivated and boorish, the mark of "new" wealth. Today there is hardly any behavior too outrageous to be considered boorish, as long as one is wealthy, powerful, or famous. When a rock star destroys his hotel room it only adds to his charisma and sells more records. When a chief executive builds a reputation for humiliating and belittling his subordinates he is considered decisive and tough. His pay goes up.

But no one achieves success alone. Our parents, our teachers, our friends, our family, our colleagues, our employees, our customers, even our competitors, all contributed in some way to our success. The list could go on and on. In the most profound sense, it can come to include the whole world and everything in it. That is the Buddhist view.

UNDERSTANDING INTERDEPENDENCE

In my Buddhist monastery, we recited a chant before every meal that began with the words "Seventy-two labors brought us this food. We should know how it comes to us." This is a chant about the work people do and how it affects and benefits us. The seventy-two labors represent all the multitude of efforts and influences that produce the food we eat, from the earthworms that loosen the soil, to the ants and snails that leaven it, to the birds and insects that pollinate it, all the way up to the farmers that plant and till it, the beasts of burden (or machinery) that harvest it, and the merchants that transport it and sell it.

In preindustrial times, the average person had a firsthand understanding of all these labors. In fact, I read recently that until World War II, more than three-fourths of the food Americans ate was grown and produced locally by friends and neighbors. These days, the net of Interdependence is so complex that hardly anyone can keep track of it all. The invention of the assembly line symbolizes modern work. By analyzing a complex task into its component parts and assigning a different worker to each part, jobs could be done more efficiently. Chances are that the job you do is some version of an assembly line. You contribute some small piece toward a greater whole.

The benefits of such efficiency are obvious. When we walk into our local supermarket, the array of fruits, vegetables, frozen dinners, ice creams, wines, and beers is, if you stop to think about it, nothing short of a miracle. And it all arrives like clockwork every day, because each worker in the vast machinery of food distribution does his or her tiny piece of an enormous job.

We all benefit from such elaborate systems, which, in the last ten or fifteen years, have stretched to cover the entire globe. This new global economy is the latest step in a process of increasing commercial complexity that has been going on for several centuries. However, there is a spiritual cost to all this specialization. What is lost when the activities that support and feed our life are so broken up and scattered is the sense of the whole.

Perceiving wholeness is something for which human beings have an innate talent. We are naturals at it. It is how we have evolved. When our ancestors looked out on the savanna, with its multitude of different plants and animals all coexisting together, it was clear to them where they themselves fit into the landscape, what things nourished them, and what they needed to do to survive. We have sacrificed that sense of wholeness by breaking up our world into so many efficient, component parts, and I think we are only beginning to understand the costs to ourselves, our society, and our children.

This wholeness does not just mean that everything is connected to everything else, but more profoundly, that in each thing, each person we encounter, the whole is expressed and reflected. This is the deeper meaning of Interdependence and the way it connects with gratitude and with our own personal spiritual practice.

THE JEWEL NET OF INDRA

Buddhism contains a beautiful metaphor for this kind of Interdependence, called the Jewel Net of Indra.

Imagine, the Buddhist texts say, a vast net, like a fisherman's net, in which each knot in the net is a diamond. Imagine this net arrayed in space, like stars and galaxies, extending in all directions. Now imagine that you come closer to the net, so close that you can peer into the heart of one individual diamond. What do you see? In that single diamond, you see the reflection of the whole net. If you shift to the next diamond in the net and look in, you see it again—the entire net is contained and reflected by every jewel in it.

Now imagine that instead of standing outside the net and seeing it as an observer you are part of it. Imagine that you yourself are one of the jewels in the net, and that every person in the world is, like you, a shining jewel. Each one of us reflects all the others. When you look into the eyes of your companion, you see yourself and everyone else. When she looks into yours, she sees the same thing.

This extraordinary visualization of the way the world works was created more than two thousand years ago by anonymous monks who spent their whole lives studying consciousness. It was created before modern physics, before the theory of relativity, before ecology and the environmental movement, before the theory of evolution. And yet the Jewel Net of Indra is astonishingly prescient in anticipating all of these scientific discoveries. It is not just Buddhism that understands the world in this way; it is how we are all coming to understand it. Modern physicists even go so far as to mathematically describe how each atomic particle in the universe influences every other one, even across light-years.

SEEING THE JEWEL IN THE FOREHEAD

If the Jewel Net is to be more than an inspirational image, how can it function practically? How can it help us get through our workday? What is the practical consequence of the realization that when we see the diamond that is another person, we simultaneously see ourselves and everyone else?

One feeling that can arise from this awareness is a sense that beneath the surface relationship we have with our coworkers, there is a more fundamental sense that they are a part of our success and we are a part of theirs. This is not a surface gratitude, or ordinary thankfulness. It is not a matter of thanking your colleague for helping you rearrange your office. The kind of gratitude you see in the Jewel Net is more unconditional than that. It is the feeling that because you are here, your fellow workers are there, and because they are there, you are here. It is also a sense that beneath our surface differences, there is the basic humanity that we all share.

One spiritual practice that can bring this awareness to life is the practice of Seeing a Jewel. Imagining that everyone is a jewel in a vast net is an inspiring metaphor, but it can also be a daily practice. As you go through your workday, try every so often to see the people around you as though they had a shining jewel in their foreheads. Be subtle. Don't stare fixedly at the forehead of the person you are talking to, and don't squint your eyes as though actually trying to see the jewel. This is a visualization practice. The jewel is in your mind's eye. You see it because you choose to see it, because it gratifies you to see it.

If you find it odd or unnatural to try to see a jewel in people's foreheads, try instead to see them as a Buddha, a spiritually awakened being. And if even an image of a Buddha is uncomfortable for you because of your religious beliefs, try to see them as a saint, or as a person of righteousness, whether they are or not. (Especially if they are not!) Try to imagine their inner nature, their soul, if you will, as radiant and jewel-like, infinitely precious and holy, like the feeling we have when we gaze down on a newborn baby. The innocence and freshness of that miracle of birth is unmistakable. We don't really lose that quality of the miraculous as we grow older—it just becomes overladen with personality, history, and emotion. We are all still newborn babies under the skin. How is it that we find it so hard to treat each other that way?

We need not limit this visualization to people. Try visualizing a jewel on the ground, in the parking lot, next to the bits of styrofoam and broken glass that litter the pavement. See if you can spot a diamond deep inside the glass of the copy machine as you slip your document in.

The office environment lacks the poetry of a natural landscape. But if you think that a grand vista such as Yellowstone Park or Yosemite is different from your fluorescent-lighted, plastic-coated cubicle, then you have forgotten the message of the Jewel Net. Peer deeply enough at Yosemite's Half Dome Mountain and you will see your cubicle. Look at your cubicle with the right slant to your vision and you can see the hazy clouds in a mountain sky. These acts of spiritual intention can transform your mundane workplace into a landscape of spiritual discovery.

The Jewel Net is everywhere.

NOTICING "THANK YOU"

Another practice that can help foster an awareness of Interdependence in the workplace is noticing whenever you or anyone else says "thank you."

Those two words come so readily and mechanically to our lips that making them more conscious requires special effort. You may be surprised, if you try this practice for a few days, how often those two words come up in conversation, and how little we really notice it. See if you can put a mental tag in your mind so that whenever you hear or speak those words—"thank you"—something awakens, notes, and silently nods. There it is again, you say to yourself, those two words, interwoven into daily discourse and ordinary politeness, but a signpost to a deeper reality.

And whenever you yourself say the words "thank you," see if you can step back from the habitual cadence of talking and say them with a little more depth and feeling. Yes, I automatically say thank you to you when you hand me the phone at work, but I can also be thankful for your presence, for all the people here, for this job, for the freedoms that I have, for my health, for this world, for everything. There is a religious movement in Japan, based partly on Buddhism, whose main spiritual practice is to say "Thank you!" with as much sincerity and frequency as possible. In that religion those two words are a universal prayer.

See if you can take these two simple spiritual tools—the words "thank you" and the image of a bright, reflective diamond—around with you in the course of your workday. See if you can use them to brighten up your mind and gladden your heart. The hustle and bustle of the workday is your surface reality, but the Jewel Net is the way things really are. Or, as my teacher used to say, "Things as it is," rebuffing all those who attempted to improve his grammar because to his spiritual eye, that was the only way to say it.

There are many things in the world, some good, some bad, some harmonious, some destructive. But there is only one Jewel Net, and everything you see and hear is already in it.

"Things as it is" is another way of saying gratitude, of saying "thank you."

Whatever you may feel about your job, the company you work for, and your boss and your coworkers, your job supports you, feeds you, helps you, and gives you an opportunity to keep growing and finding fresh chances.

THE PRACTICE OF BEING GRATEFUL

We have spoken earlier about antidotes—the Half Smile as an antidote to anger, kindness as a response to an adversary, patience and listening as an antidote to control. Gratitude can function as an antidote too. Here is a simple practice you can do. Whenever you find yourself in a grumpy, complaining mood, immediately think of something to be grateful for. You might even try to think of *ten* things to be grateful for. That takes some time. Take the time to enunciate each thing slowly:

My family.

Good health.

My good friend.

A regular paycheck.

The air I breathe.

And so on. By then, you might have completely forgotten what was making you grumpy!

What is interesting about this practice is that it is not at all difficult. If I were to ask you now to pause in your reading and think of two or three things to be grateful for, I'm sure you would have no difficulty. The reality of gratitude is so strong, so deeply present in our lives, that shifting the attention to gratitude is one of the most reliable ways to alter your state of mind. If you do it every day, it is interesting to see how the list changes, how often something that just happened—some small kindness or unexpected pleasure in the course of our day—spontaneously makes it onto the list.

And if you have achieved real success in your work, if everything is going well for you, then by all means be sure to include that fact close to the top of your list. So many people would like to be in your shoes and have what you have. What you have achieved is special, but it is not your unique personal property. It is the result of many causes. The most appropriate response to that fact is to be grateful.

One of the most common spiritual practices is saying grace at meals—an important practice for Buddhists as well as Christians and Jews. But in a larger sense, every moment is a meal, every occasion nourishes us. Our work, which gives us livelihood, is as much nourishment as any feast. In that sense, we might say grace before every workday, giving thanks for everything that makes our work successful and satisfying. At the very end of the book, I describe a visualization practice that does that.

INTERDEPENDENCE AND
RIGHT LIVELIHOOD

As a final reflection on Interdependence in the workplace, let's consider Right Livelihood. The Buddhist teaching of Right Livelihood refers to an occupation that causes a minimum of harm and suffering to other beings, whether human, plant, or animal. For traditional Buddhists, occupations such as butcher, tanner, and soldier were to be avoided, since such work was connected with the killing of other beings. For Buddhist monks, even farming was forbidden because tilling the soil caused harm to the creatures that lived there, such as insects and worms.

This kind of teaching made sense in the ancient world, where there was a clear division of spiritual roles. The laypeople worked hard to support themselves and their families, and the monks did their part by "working" on spiritual matters. Right Livelihood is still a powerful teaching for today's world. For example, is it all right to make one's living cutting down trees in an area where endangered species live? Or to burn tropical rain forests to make farmland? Or to manufacture pesticides that pollute rivers and streams? These are pressing political, ethical, and spiritual questions as fresh and timely as today's headlines. We might say that the practical consequences of a livelihood that harms, first pointed out by the Buddha more than two millennia ago, have now reached a critical point where they affect everyone.

Certainly a slaughterhouse worker is more directly connected with killing than a schoolteacher. The chairman of an oil company has more direct responsibility for the introduction of harmful substances into the environment than a violin maker. But in reality, we all participate in harm to other beings to one degree or another. If we read a newspaper, we are supporting the destruction of forests. If we use soap, a river somewhere becomes more polluted so that we can be more clean. There is no escape from this Interdependence.

Some of my Buddhist friends scrutinize their purchases and actions carefully, to minimize this kind of collusion. They refuse to work for, purchase from, or invest in companies that pollute or harm. They don't wear leather; they don't eat meat. They use paper rather than plastic (although paper mills pollute too). They recycle their bottles and cans. This is a wonderful effort. If all of us lived that way, it would begin to alter the dynamics of our consumer economy and force manufacturers to change their business practices. The growth of the organic food industry is a good example of how consumer consciousness has created new markets as well as better health. At the same time, we must remember that for many working people on a budget, organic food is a difficult-to-afford luxury.

That is one reason I do not want to be in the business of ranking occupations on a scale of "right" and "not-so-right": Like organic food, job choice is a luxury that many working people can ill afford. The ability to choose one's line of work tends to be confined to people with education, social skills, and marketable expertise. For many people, just to have a job at all, any job, is accomplishment enough. We must remember that not having a job is also a cause for suffering and harm, not only to the unemployed person but to that person's family, children, and friends.

We must all share responsibility for the kind of world we have created. If our world is to change, if it is to become more humane, less destructive, and more careful of resources, environment, and living beings, then the real change will have to come from within ourselves. When enough of us are ready to live differently, to bring spiritual values to the forefront of our priorities, then a deeper transformation of livelihood can truly begin.

In the meantime, my approach to Right Livelihood is to take the right-versus-wrong out of the equation and to instead emphasize *conscious* livelihood. Instead of making judgments about the work people do and ranking it on some scale of spiritual acceptability, I emphasize being more conscious and aware of what we are doing at work. It is certainly possible that this may result in our being unwilling to continue our current occupation and seeking another one. Someone who works for a tobacco company, for example, who closely examines the consequences of tobacco products for our society, may find that he cannot continue. But one of the main reasons that the tobacco industry is now finally being held accountable for its harm is the courageous actions of tobacco company employees who came forward with documents and evidence. If those employees had all left, there would have been no one to tell the world the truth. This is yet another example of the distinction we made at the beginning of this section between success and Accomplishment. Many of those whistle-blowers sacrificed job success for their principles. Indeed, some of them were fired! But out of all the tens of thousands of tobacco industry workers, which ones will grow old with the knowledge that when it really mattered, they did the right thing?

When I was still active as a Buddhist priest, I was approached after my weekly sermon by a man who, with some hesitation, revealed that he was a policeman. He was also a Buddhist but needed to keep that fact a secret from his colleagues. He wanted to know whether I thought a Buddhist should be a policeman.

I thought about it for a moment and replied, "Well, I'm not sure I would be comfortable carrying a gun and having the responsibility of using deadly force."

As I got to know the man, I appreciated how difficult his job was and how glad I was that he was willing to do it. Who would I rather have holding the gun, a person who had given little thought to the deeper issues of crime, transgression, and protection from harm, or someone like this man, who had thought about them a great deal?

Much later, the man confided in me that our conversation had been a turning point in his willingness to continue in his profession. He appreciated my candor in expressing my own reservations, which matched his own. Because I had doubt but was not dogmatic or judgmental, he said, that encouraged him.

The most important part of Right Livelihood, I think, is not the "right," but the livelihood itself. There was a time in the not-so-distant human past when there was no such thing as a job, only hunting, gathering, farming, and some essential toolmaking. As work has become more and more specialized and divorced from its original purpose, it has become more difficult to endow work with intrinsic meaning and spiritual worth. Not too long ago, a shoemaker could walk the streets of his village and see the fruit of his craft on the feet of everyone who passed. His pride in his workmanship was not an abstraction. It was part and parcel of his personal relationships, his place in the community, and, ultimately, his place with God.

When your job is to process credit applications for a multinational financial conglomerate, where is that pride? Where is that accomplishment? Where is that connection? It no longer comes ready-made with the job. You have to create it out of your own resources, effort, and sense of self-respect.

The primary purpose of this book is not to change the world. It is not to transform the workplace, or commerce, or the nature of work. It is not even to transform organizations. Its primary purpose is to transform individuals.

If by transforming one person, this book contributes to the transformation of work, society, and commerce, then that is fine. When that person enters her workplace with the resolve to be more conscious and aware in her work, to treat her coworkers with more care and compassion, and to treat the stresses and strains that come with her job as opportunities to grow inwardly and develop, then she has already achieved Right Livelihood.

PRACTICES FOR GRATITUDE

- Try to see everyone at work as a diamond in a vast Jewel Net. As an act of conscious visualization, imagine a diamond in the forehead of each of your coworkers.

- Notice when you say or someone near you says "Thank you." Think of those two words as a signpost to the spiritual world.

- Whenever you are in a negative frame of mind, think of one, two, three, or even ten things to be grateful for. Here are some examples to start:
  Breath.
  Health.
  Food.
  A friend.

C an you handle power?

If you can, then you are a rare person. Most people have trouble with power. Power is a great seducer and corrupter. Lord Acton's dictum about power—"Power tends to corrupt, and absolute power corrupts absolutely"—is so frequently cited it has become a cliché. When those words were written, kings and emperors still did wield absolute power. That is less true today, but power still corrupts, and in the workplace,

power, like money, is always an issue. Very few workplaces are run as democracies. Even the ones that claim to be are often not as democratic as they seem. I have worked both for idealistic, nonprofit organizations and for profit-making corporations, and the main difference I have seen is that in the profit sector, the power relationships are more visible and straightforward.

At first blush power seems to be a high-energy state. The manager who shouts and pounds on the table to get his way may seem to be wielding power. The policeman whose whistle screeches at you as he stops you from crossing the street is wielding power. But if you have ever spent time with someone who has *real* power, the energy is usually quiet and subtle. I once made a presentation at a

The power of Integrity is based on a firm inner sense of values that allows you to stand your ground regardless of what you are doing or where you are.

two-billion-dollar company. Halfway through my presentation, the CEO came in and sat in the back. He said nothing, but the feeling of everyone in the room changed markedly. We were in the presence of power. The shouting manager is not wielding power, he is frustrated because he doesn't have power. Real power is quiet. And Inner Power, which is the subject of this chapter, is the most quiet of all. It is nearly invisible, but it can move mountains.

In the Buddhist scripture, there was once an evil monk who repeatedly plotted to kill the Buddha. In one of his attempts, he fed an elephant liquor to make it intoxicated and sent it charging toward the Buddha. But when the elephant confronted the calm countenance of the Buddha, who made no effort to get out of the way, it became docile and knelt down in front of the Buddha to be petted.

Even animals, the story tells us, are responsive to the effect of Inner Power.

KINDS OF POWER

There are many kinds of power, many ways that one person has of bending another to his will. Of course, the ultimate power is deadly force. Although that power is still exercised all over the world by nations against other nations and by oppressive governments against their citizens, thankfully our supervisors at work don't hold whips in their hands and point shotguns at us. Slavery and serfdom are relics of a crueler past. The kinds of power we encounter at work are more subtle than that.

Preeminent in a capitalist system is the power of ownership. The owners, or the shareholders, rule supreme. I lost my job once because the ultimate owner of the company I worked for was a conglomerate in Japan. The executives in Japan had never met me and knew very little about the company I worked for, except for a few sheets of paper that summarized our disappointing earnings. Yet they had the power to disrupt my livelihood from across the ocean.

In most companies of any size, the power of rank comes next. The president, CEO, or boss is vested with considerable power over others—to hire and fire, to promote or demote, to offer or withhold a bonus or raise. If you are a manager or boss, you wield that power. You may be the nicest person in the world, and your subordinates may tell you that they like and respect you, but to some extent, they are cautious with you. You have power.

There are other flavors of workplace power. Knowledge is power, particularly in our high-tech world. When the computers go down, everything comes to a halt, until the system administrators, whose specialized skills hold the rest of the company hostage, can bring the system back online.

Money is power. Some think it is the supreme power. I once knew a member of a European aristocratic family, a distinguished lady in her sixties. One day, when we were talking about her experiences during World War II, she said, "Let me tell you a secret. No matter what anyone tells you, wars are always about money!" I don't know if that's always true, but I have long remembered her remark. It may be truer than we would like to believe.

Physical beauty confers power. For a movie star or a model, beauty can be worth millions and launch a whole career. One's physical bearing and presence can often be an important ingredient in one's ability to influence others. I once read a study that surveyed the physical height of male chief executives and found that on average they were three to four inches taller than the average male adult. That was an old study. With the increasing diversity of chief executives (many of whom are now women), this statistic is less important than it once was. But physical presence and appearance count for more than we would like to admit.

Information is increasingly a profound source of power. An attendee at one of my workshops said that at one time she was a compensation specialist for a Fortune 500 company. She had access to everyone's salary information—who got what bonuses, who got raises and who didn't, as well as the stock-option plans of the top executives. She told us how she would walk through a room and wonder what effect it would have on two people who sat side by side doing the same job if she told them that one made twenty thousand dollars a year more than the other.

"Did anyone ever offer you a bribe to spill the beans?" someone asked.

She nodded vigorously. "You wouldn't believe the things people said to me."

That's the power of information.

WHY POWER CORRUPTS

What is it about power that tends to bring out the worst in us? Why does it so often happen that when we take the best worker on a team and make him a supervisor, he turns into a petty tyrant overnight? It is the same person, with the same good qualities that earned him the promotion. But in the exercise of newfound power a shadow emerges, a darker side of our nature. What is that all about?

We all have a deep desire to be in control, to be safe and secure, to be free from worry and anxiety. That need is one of the deepest forces underlying all our thoughts and actions. Even though as responsible, mature adults, we know that we cannot live forever, we cannot get everything we want, we cannot be continuously happy, and we will suffer pain, misfortune, and disappointment in the course of our life, this does not stop us from wanting to be free from all of that.

In other words, the child in each of us wants to be the star of a fairy tale in which every wish comes true. To want that, even though intellectually we know we cannot have it, is what Buddhists call grasping, or clinging. We needn't be ashamed to admit we feel this way. We all do. It is the human condition.

That is why power corrupts us. Power gives us the illusion that we can come a bit closer to that fairy-tale dream, that we can control our circumstances to block out unpleasantness, to avoid difficulty and pain. And it is not entirely illusion. If you are wealthy, you have the power to avoid many of life's ordinary inconveniences. You never have to pick up your own dry cleaning. You don't have to hassle with rush-hour traffic—you can hire a limousine. And if the freeways are really snarled, you can hire a helicopter. Or perhaps you own a helicopter!

I have succumbed to some of these temptations. When I was a Buddhist monk, I lived through the winter without heat. I walked more than I drove. I ate a spare, simple diet. I saw these modest hardships as part of my spiritual training, so they didn't bother me. Now, during my business travels, I find myself becoming irritated if the hotel I'm staying at is noisy, if I have a middle seat on the airplane, or if the restaurant service is slow. Because I am living a life of more wealth, and more seeming control, my state of mind is actually less resilient and less accepting than when I was a monk. Because I have more Outer Power, I am tempted to use it to make my life more protected and smooth. But it has the opposite effect. Instead, I have less Inner Power. I am more vulnerable and weak.

Power is an illusion, but a very convincing one. We have built an entire society around the premise that power, particularly the power of money, is a good thing. According to the images that bombard us from every television screen, there is no more exciting, glamorous life than a life filled with money and power.

GOOD BOSS, BAD BOSS

A good friend who was reading the manuscript of this book remarked, "You don't seem to portray bosses in a very good light." I considered her remark and concluded that she was probably right. There are good bosses and bad bosses, but I think most people have difficulty with their boss at some time in their career. Another friend, who owns his own company, was a guest speaker at a nearby business school. "How many of you have had good bosses?" he asked the class of about fifty. A few hands were raised. "How many of you have had bosses from hell?" More than half the class raised their hands.

Aside from the intrinsic corruption of power, most people in management receive little, if any, training about how to manage power and its corruptions. Through whatever means, trained or not, people rise to power, wield power, and in many cases abuse power. If bosses don't do their jobs well, it is not because they are bad people, but because organizations don't train them in how to cope with power or provide them with a system of values that puts power in perspective.

THE POWER OF INTEGRITY

The kinds of powers I have listed thus far are unrelated to character. James Hillman has studied power in his book *Kinds of Power*. In addition to those I have already mentioned, he explores one more, which he calls Purism. Purism, exemplified by such leaders as Martin Luther King Jr. and Gandhi, is quite different from other kinds of power. The power of Purism, which I would call Integrity, is based not on any outward rank, or wealth, or knowledge, or beauty, but on character, a firm inner sense of values that allows you to stand your ground regardless of what you are doing or where you are.

Gandhi is a good example. The culminating moment of India's struggle for independence came when Gandhi arrived, alone, at the viceroy's palace to negotiate with the British Empire for independence. In the cinematic version of this moment (with Ben Kingsley in the title role), Gandhi slowly walks up the steps, unclothed except for his loincloth, as the viceroy and his aides peer fretfully from behind the curtains. "Here he comes!" the viceroy mutters, fearful of the incorruptible power of this gaunt, barefoot old man.

That is the power of Integrity. It is, according to Dr. Hillman, a more potent force than any other kind of power, because it is unconditional and driven entirely from within. That is why so many spiritual heroes, such as Gandhi, die by assassination. Death is the only thing that stops them.

OUTER AND INNER POWER

All the kinds of powers I have mentioned, except for the power of Integrity, fall into the category of Outer Power. Outer Power is relative. For it to function, some people must have more than others. The president of your company has more power than you. You have more power than the janitor who sweeps the floors. The janitor has more power than the homeless person on the street outside. The homeless person has more power than a stray dog.

The hierarchy of Outer Power is changeable. You are a rising star one day, old news the next. A new management team comes in with fresh-scrubbed faces and bright ideas. A year later the stock price has sagged and they are all sacked. This year the value of your stock options soars, and you think about early retirement. Next year the company is on the ropes, and you worry about keeping your job.

The games that people play with power in the workplace can be the least pleasant aspects of working. Many people who come to my workshops have either left large corporations or are thinking about doing so. When I ask what is the most difficult part of their work life, they often say, "The politics."

The jockeying for power and influence within a company is certainly not an example of human beings at their best, but it reflects the reality of organizational life. The conventional wisdom is that workplace competition brings out the best in people. While internal competition may be good for companies, it takes a large toll on human relationships. That is why I feel it is so important to cultivate not just Outer Power, which leads to conventional workplace success, but Inner Power, which leads to true Accomplishment and spiritual satisfaction.

People used to think that there was some relationship between Inner and Outer Power, that if they worked hard, were loyal to their company, were honest and fair in their dealings with people, then they would be rewarded with continued employment, promotions, status, and recognition. One of the big changes of the last ten years has been the breakdown of that system. Our economy is now global. Even the heads of companies are not masters of their own fate. Not just our own country, but the whole world is going through wrenching change, and the old days of a steady job and a secure future are probably gone forever. In the face of such rapid change, what is the lowly individual worker, struggling to maintain predictability and security in his or her life, to do? Today people have to take responsibility for their own future rather than rely on their employer to do it for them. This means they need to become more independent, more able to stand on their own, both in a material and a spiritual sense.

CULTIVATING INNER POWER

Many of the practices and techniques described in this book are actually ways of cultivating Inner Power. In fact, every time I have said "You are the boss of your inner life" I am affirming Inner Power. Whenever we make spiritual intention conscious, whenever we capture a moment of awareness from the constant distractions of our job, we are scoring a point for Inner Power.

To make this more explicit, you might experiment by making two lists: one of all the areas where you feel you do have power on the job and another of all those where you feel you do not. Such a list might look like this:

HAVE POWER

I'm the only one with supervisor privileges to the network.
I set the strategic direction for my area.
I manage fourteen people in my department.
I have a discretionary annual budget of $172,000.
I can promote or demote, give bonuses or withhold them.

DO NOT HAVE POWER

I don't set my own salary.
I can't control how well the company as a whole will do.
I can't control whether my boss is in one of his bad moods.
I can't guarantee whether or not my team will perform as well as I would like.
I can't force anyone else at the workplace to like me.

And then, next to the list of "Do Not Have Power" items, see if you can think of acts of Inner Power that complement each one. For example, next to "I don't set my own salary" you can put "But I have Inner Power over my attitude toward money." And next to "I can't force anyone else at the workplace to like me" you can put "I have Inner Power over the kindness and respect with which I treat my colleagues."

One test of whether you are relying on Inner rather than Outer Power is the feeling of the energy. As we mentioned earlier, Inner Power is quiet, like the trunk of an ancient tree, whereas Outer Power is hot and noisy, like a lawnmower or a television playing loudly. The Hot Positive energies of Conflict—anger, fear, anxiety, worry—are the psyche's effort to mobilize some power in a situation where we feel insecure or helpless. But when you can say, for example (either silently or out loud), "I am really angry here" rather than "Damn it!" Inner Power has come to the fore and, in a sense, turned to your hot anger and said, "Thanks. I can take it from here."

This kind of shift has been an important practice for me. My mental quickness is definitely a form of Outer Power, which I can use to dominate and control situations. When I get a piece of bad news in my business, my first instinct is to pick up the phone and launch into action. But I know now that while that reaction can often be superficially effective, in the long run it doesn't work nearly as well as patience, deliberation, and paying attention to all the things that start happening when I *don't* immediately act. It is true that a small percentage of the time, maybe 10 percent, the rapid response *is* the best one, such as when the stove catches fire. It is for these circumstances that our reactive emotions, like fear and anger, have evolved to help us.

CHARACTER AND TEMPTATION

Character is the key to these transformations. The more we can rely on character, the more we make it the touchstone of how we live our life, the less we are at the mercy of outside events and forces. The more how we feel about ourselves and our situation is rooted in something inside rather than something outside, the better our work life will be, and the less we will feel a victim of our circumstances.

To have Inner Power means that regardless of the chaos and changing circumstances around you, you have somewhere solid to stand. You know who you are. Personal integrity has taken quite a beating in recent years, not only in the business world but everywhere. A high percentage of college students report that they regularly cheat. Workers who feel less commitment from their employer reciprocate by cutting corners on their job.

Remember Matsu, the star of the movie *Rickshaw Man*? Later in the movie, there is a scene where Matsu is assigned to take an army general across town. The general asks him, "Do you know the way?" Matsu replies, "Of course." The general asks again, "Are you sure you know where to take me?" Matsu replies, "Sure! How many times do I have to tell you?" The general's attaché leaps forward to beat Matsu to the ground. But the general waves him off with a smile. As a military man, he is impressed with Matsu's spirit, his Inner Power. He likes the fact that no one, not even a general, can push him around. He nods to Matsu to proceed.

It may seem old-fashioned to emphasize a return to spiritual values as a way to cope with the workplace, but it is the only resource that no one can take away from us. In addition, the bulk of the negative experiences we have at work, even those that are no fault of our own—the stress, the anger and worry, the fear, the boredom, and the discouragement—are exacerbated by a lack of Inner Power. When we can stand our ground, anger and fear do not loom as large for us, and the actions of others, even our superiors, are not as threatening. The more we can reach within for solace and sustenance, the less the irritations of the workplace will bother us. The more we can keep returning to the fundamentals of our spiritual life, the less the temptations of workplace success will corrupt us.

That is why the life histories of great spiritual teachers include a moment of great temptation, a time when the lure of Outer Power seems about to prevail. When Satan tempted Jesus in the wilderness, offering him the whole world in exchange for his allegiance, Jesus was tempted. But in the end, he stood his ground, and it was Satan who yielded. When the Buddha was deep in meditation under the tree of enlightenment, Mara, the Lord of Illusion, tempted the Buddha with beautiful maidens, with hailstorms, with doubt. And when that failed, Mara challenged the Buddha, saying, "Get up from that seat. I, the Lord of Illusion, rule the world. I own that seat, not you."

In response, the Buddha reached out and touched the ground with his fingertips. "You may own the whole world, Mara," the Buddha replied. "But this place where I sit belongs to me and I cannot be moved from it." The earth itself quaked in agreement. With that, Mara was defeated. He knew that the Buddha was right. To this day, Buddha statues the world over portray this moment by showing the Buddha's right hand stretched forward in the so-called earth-touching posture.

Gandhi used that same Inner Power against the British. He had no weapons, no armies, no wealth of empire. All he had were his convictions and the trust of his millions of loyal followers, who, in the face of clubs, whips, and gunfire, would not be moved.

At the very least, Inner Power will give you the fortitude to negotiate the thicket of workplace uncertainties. In situations of real adversity, it may mean the difference between triumph and defeat. And if you are at the top of your game, if your work life is fulfilling and satisfying and you cannot imagine how you could improve it, then Inner Power will give you the perspective not to be complacent, arrogant, or overly proud.

Though the modern workplace is a recent invention and continues to grow and change, the spiritual values that I have been talking about throughout this book are very old, as old as humanity itself. In the history of ancient India or Judea, ancient Greece or Rome, the human dramas are much the same as those today. Anger, greed, temptation, arrogance, and ambition coexisted in uneasy balance with generosity, integrity, honesty, compassion, and forgiveness. Our fourfold Energy Wheel of Conflict, Stagnation, Inspiration, and Accomplishment reflects those ancient worlds as aptly as it does ours.

Outer Power comes and goes. Inner Power, once gained, stays with you your whole life. You may think that the modern workplace has no place for timeless spiritual values, that it brushes them aside

242 · Work as a Spiritual Practice

as irrelevant to the goals of efficiency and profit. That's how it may seem, but it is not really so. That's what Mara thought too, but he was mistaken. Inner Power is stronger.

PRACTICES FOR POWER

- Make a list of areas in your work where you have power and areas where you do not. Complement the "don't have power" list with ways that Inner Power can substitute.

- What are the different kinds of Outer Power at work in your workplace? Which ones do you wield? How?

- Reflect on instances on the job where Inner Power has come to the fore. What did the energy feel like? How did it differ from the feeling of Outer Power?

part six

FINAL THOUGHTS

I have said before that I am not out to change organizations but to transform individuals. It is not that I don't want to see organizations change, but I'm not sure how to do it in a way that lasts. Even when a company has a visionary CEO, a person who transforms the company culture by force of conviction, such leaders come and go. Companies are bought and sold. Profits rise and fall. There is no permanence to organizational culture.

I once attended a workshop on Total

Quality Management with Dr. W. Edwards Deming, the man credited with bringing quality control to Japan after World War II. Dr. Deming was adamant about how organizations change. "Change comes from the top!" he said. When someone asked him to define what he meant by top, Deming leaned into the microphone and bellowed, "Top means top!" He meant the president or CEO. But the average CEO's tenure, according to a recent business study, is three and a half years, barely enough time to start making changes before a new "top" comes in! I was in the process of instituting Dr. Deming's philosophy at my last job, with the full support of the president and the board, when the company was sold. The new owners saw quality management as a fad. I was out of a job.

When we believe that the world makes us, that it determines what we can and cannot do, then we see ourselves as small and weak. But when we understand that we make the world— individually and together—then we become formidable and strong.

Nevertheless, organizations and societies are the sum total of all the individuals in them. To transform one person is to begin the process of transforming many people. If our modern workplace is to become more humane, caring, and devoted to the well-being of people and less obsessed with short-term efficiency and profit, then that larger transformation must begin one person at a time. Remember the Jewel Net of Indra? One person's diamond reflects the whole net.

The workplace reflects the values and priorities of the larger society. Our system of free-market capitalism creates jobs and defines their purpose, which is to produce wealth and generate profit. And even in the nonprofit sector—in education, in healthcare and social services, even in government—the mentality of for-profit efficiency is increasingly the norm.

There is a reason why our system has eclipsed all other alternatives, such as communism, European-style socialism, and Asian centrally controlled economies. The free market is flexible. It empowers individuals, encourages innovation and risk taking, and brings out the best in people (though some would argue that it also brings out the worst). Ten years ago, it was the Japanese-style corporate model that was seen as the world's future. Today, the American economic system is the envy of the world. It remains to be seen whether our dominance will continue or fall victim to yet another turn in the road.

My own case is an argument for the American model. I was able to leave my old job with some severance pay, a good idea for a product, some skills and energy, and create not only a viable business but several new jobs. I didn't have to ask anyone's permission. I didn't have to bribe government bureaucrats or placate organized criminals; I didn't even need much money. In another part of the world, under another system of economics, I wouldn't have been able to do that. There wouldn't have been any incentive for me to take that risk. Under communism, my effort would probably have been considered a crime.

Those who think of General Motors and Microsoft as the exemplars of capitalism must remember that much of capitalism's wealth and job creation is fueled not by Fortune 500 corporations but by small businesses. At the personal, entrepreneurial level, capitalism looks like a good thing. But it suffers from a number of shortcomings, including the lack of a moral compass. For example, from the purely economic perspective, the tobacco company and the manufacturer of the heart-lung machine are equivalent. Both satisfy a market need. Both add to the gross national product. Both produce jobs. The fact that the tobacco company's product takes lives and the heart-lung machine saves them is outside the economist's purview. (After forty years of effort by the anti-tobacco movement, tobacco's real costs to society are at last becoming visible and are being dealt with by legislation. But it has taken a long time.)

Another problem with capitalism is that while it rewards success, it does not protect against failure. In fact, the nature of the game is that for there to be winners, there must be losers. Today's papers are full of Japan's economic woes, with American pundits urging the Japanese to accept a higher unemployment rate in order to be more efficient, more like us. The pundits may be right, but what about all those unemployed Japanese workers and their families? It is one thing if capitalism's losers are entrepreneurs like me, who consciously accept risks in the hope of gain. But what about the whole factory of people who are laid off because of a blip in the global financial markets, or because workers in Malaysia will do the same work for a dollar a day? It isn't enough to say "They knew the risks." If it is *your* job that is erased, if it is your family's well-being that is in danger, that is small consolation. We are emerging from a long period where government, with its unemployment and welfare programs, was expected to provide the safety net. The cries to "end welfare as we know it" resonate well politically but do little to assure that those cast out of the safety net can actually find jobs. Whether or not those jobs exist is not up to government but to the market, which may have other priorities.

Some may argue that an acceptance of winners and losers is precisely what countries such as Japan need to become more competitive in today's global economy, and that the painful layoffs in the United States in the early 1990s are precisely what has positioned our economy to be dominant now. Ten years ago, Japan's old system of lifetime employment was being touted as the future. Now the pundits have consigned it to the dustbin of history. Maybe the deeper truth is that we are all in the middle of a long-term global experiment about the kind of society we want, and no one yet knows the outcome.

The fact that other economic systems have faltered does not mean that our system is without flaw. To paraphrase Winston Churchill's definition of democracy, free-market capitalism is the worst system there is, except for all the others. We have learned how to create economic freedom, but we have not yet mastered how to ensure economic justice. We are the wealthiest generation in human history, but are we the wisest? And what will happen now that everyone else in the world wants to be just like us, with our three televisions, two cars, and a personal monthly energy bill greater than the annual income per capita of some poor countries? Can the planet sustain us, or are the three-legged frogs now cropping up in freshwater ponds all over America one of many warning signs that it cannot?

I hasten to add that while I do not have three televisions (only one, on which I enjoy watching *Seinfeld* reruns, Jim Lehrer, and baseball), I do have two cars, three home computers, a Steinway grand piano, and a comfortable home. I cherish the time to compose and play music, I love going to the movies, and once a day I brew a cup of premium coffee, even though I know I may be contributing to the destruction of shade-tree habitat in South America. Though I am clearly not an ascetic, I once did without all these things, and if need be I could do so again. These enjoyments do not define my life or my true happiness. And I cannot enjoy these things completely unless I am also willing to wish and work for that same happiness for everyone else in the world. Actually, managing planetary population is the most direct way to deal with the three-legged frogs. As the Dalai Lama himself says, "There are too many precious human beings on the earth!" But even if the world were not overpopulated, the fundamental questions would remain. How should we live as human beings? How should we organize our economic, social, and spiritual life?

When I was young, I parted ways with mainstream society in the hope that Buddhism had the answers. I now feel that it may have some, but not all. Buddhism was formed long ago, when human societies were simpler, when cities were few and the global population was a tiny fraction of what it is today. Besides, the Buddha was not primarily a social reformer, nor an architect of economic or social systems, but a contemplative. Today, as much as I appreciate the depth of Buddhism's insights, I see them as only one of many sources of wisdom that must unite to create a comprehensive solution.

One of Buddhism's key contributions is its teaching that most human suffering and injustice has its origins in desire—desire for wealth, power, security, safety, and long life. We are all, to one degree or another, prisoners of such desires. That is our human nature, and commerce is simply the collective expression of all those individual wants and needs. Whether we want a loaf of bread, a thinner nose, a faster car, an education for our child, a medicine for our pain, or an evening at a Rolling Stones concert, there is a commercial transaction that can satisfy that want.

But desires are not all equivalent. Though the desire for a loaf of bread is not the same as the desire for a Rolex watch—either materially or spiritually—our consumer society is based on the premise that it is, that any human desire worth having is worth fulfilling. The advertising industry exists primarily to stimulate these desires and in some cases to invent them out of whole cloth. Such a marketplace does not ask questions or make value judgments. Instead, it assumes that the best way to satisfy the most people is to let them all freely pursue their own self-interest. Even where the legal system draws the line—with illegal drugs, for example—that line is rather arbitrary. Nicotine is as addictive as heroin and arguably as harmful.

It has been left to spiritual leaders, such as the Buddha, to challenge our fundamental assumptions about human desire. Though known to posterity as a great spiritual teacher, the Buddha was, until the age of twenty-nine, the ancient equivalent of a billionaire, a prince of wealth and privilege. His spiritual awakening began when he realized that all his wealth and power could not provide him with true happiness. He took to traveling in disguise among the common people, where he experienced firsthand the suffering of the people whose labor was the basis of his own wealth. Shortly after that, he left the palace forever and became a wandering monk. The Buddha's core message is that human nature is not fixed. Unlike Thomas Hobbes, Adam Smith, and other Western thinkers who accepted human nature as a given and whose philosophies form the basis of modern commerce, the Buddha felt that our human nature is capable of transformation or, to be more precise, self-transformation.

If that is true, then the free market is even freer than we usually think. Suppose everyone suddenly became convinced that Rolex watches caused heart attacks. The market for Rolex watches would collapse overnight. People would throw away their old ones, nobody would buy new ones, and soon the makers of Rolex watches would be out of business. This is not just a fantasy. Such things do happen. Not too long ago, the "Alar" scare convinced consumers that apples contained a dangerous pesticide. Apple prices fell precipitously. Some apple farms nearly failed. It turned out that the scare was a false alarm, and the apples were not dangerous. But it was too late for some small farmers.

The marketplace begins in the mind.

To put it another way: The marketplace does not control us, we control the marketplace—at least to the extent that our inner values and character are stronger than the lure of advertisements and possessions. If we truly want our system of commerce and the conditions of our employment to change, then the place to start is with ourselves. The sum total of what each of us must have or can do without creates the whole economy that employs us and sustains us. If we built an economic system based more on loaves of bread and less on Rolex watches, more on compassion than on competition, more on spiritual than material values, we might end up with a very different world from the one we live in today. The contemporary Vietnamese Buddhist teacher Thich Nhat Hanh once said that if every American were to forgo one alcoholic drink and one serving of meat per week, it would feed the population of his native country for a year. What would induce us Americans to do that? Why is fasting such a common spiritual practice throughout the world? Is it because it helps to remember what is really important? The ultimate solution to the inequities and failings of free-market capitalism is not economic but spiritual. In the end, it is our own deeply held beliefs and values that create the world in which we all are fated to live.

If an emphasis on spiritual values becomes sufficiently strong among a large enough group of people, the marketplace will begin to reflect that desire. There are already some markets that are almost entirely the creation of such a shift in values, such as the organic food industry or alternative healthcare. Even meditation centers and corporate mindfulness programs are filling a market need. And what about the workplace itself? Employment operates like any other market, according to the laws of supply and demand. Right now, for example, there is a worldwide shortage of computer programmers, which accounts for their premium starting salaries and benefits. But remember the old slogan, "Suppose they gave a war and nobody came." Suppose money was no longer the prime attraction for talented, spiritually aware job seekers. My workshops are full of people for whom the lure of riches no longer suffices. For them, quality of work and quality of life are what count. And that reflects a larger trend. One research institute estimates that over the next ten years 25 percent of Americans will become "downshifters," and strive to scale their life back to some degree.

There was a time when the workweek was six days, when health benefits, flex time, maternity leave, and the host of other workplace benefits we now take for granted did not exist. Seventy-five years ago, a worker who insisted on such perquisites would have been laughed out of the boss's office and probably fired. Many business executives would argue that catering to workers' spiritual needs is going too far. I read recently of one chief executive of a midwestern firm who complained to his human resources staff about fuzzy-headed, "New Age" ideas among some middle managers. "I want you to develop a test to identify those people," he grumbled, "so we can get rid of them." I'd be willing to bet that "those people" were that firm's most talented managers.

On the other hand, some progressive companies are establishing wellness programs, yoga classes, meditation and prayer rooms, and on-site health clubs. There are now corporate training programs in mindfulness, and Buddhist meditation teachers are being recruited to lead them. Companies usually need robust earnings to support such perks, and in all likelihood such programs will be the first to be cut when profits dip. The fact that these programs exist at all is a good first step, but they are not necessarily a sign—yet—of fundamental change in the core business culture.

How many of us in business stop to ask ourselves: Why are we doing all this? What, ultimately, is the point? What is profit, really, and why is it important? All of this worldwide commercial activity is, at the end of the day, supposed to be contributing to human happiness, to contentment, to a better life for people. Otherwise, why do it? And is it really providing more happiness to more people? The vast, interconnected global economy that we have created presumably exists to satisfy at least some of these goals. Or does it? Do we control it, or does it control us? Does it exist for the benefit of everyone or only the powerful few?

And if happiness is the ultimate goal, then what is happiness, anyway? Is it just having more money in the bank? More cars in the garage, more vacation homes? Most people would agree that happiness, at root, is a spiritual, not material, value. That is what Jesus and the Buddha taught, what all great spiritual leaders taught.

But why seek to be happy? Why make a living? Why live at all? The philosopher Albert Camus began his masterpiece *The Myth of Sisyphus* by writing, "Judging whether or not life is worth living amounts to answering the fundamental question of all philosophy." Each of us, whether we realize it or not, asks ourself that question every day, and every day we make that judgment anew in favor of life. We do want to keep on living, against all odds. We even find joy in it, wherever we can.

Is it possible to imagine a world where we can expect to make more than a living, to find not just necessity in our work but joy as well? Can that be the next entitlement for workers of the twenty-first century? If that seems too much to ask, I would argue, why ask for less? That said, such a change in fundamental values and outlook will not happen quickly. It may take ten, twenty, fifty, or a hundred years. Many people in the developing world are just emerging from grinding poverty—just as Europe was a few hundred years ago. And even in the United States, the richest country on the planet, there is much poverty. People in the world's emerging nations may need to have their three televisions and two cars long enough to assure themselves that such luxuries are not the be all and end all of human existence, as the American TV channels they receive on their satellite dishes would have them believe. The Buddha himself needed twenty-nine years of the princely life before he came to that same conclusion, and he was a born sage! Materialism as the reigning creed of human existence may need to complete its life cycle just as previous belief systems have done. But in the end, it is not our worldly desires that will set the grand agenda for our long-term future as a species but our spiritual aspirations.

It is to that end that I have written this book, and it is in the service of that goal that I encourage you to believe in yourself, to trust yourself, and to demand the best of yourself and your workplace. When we believe that the world makes us, that it determines what we can and cannot do, then we see ourselves as small and weak. But when we understand that we make the world—individually and together—then we become formidable and strong. The light that radiates out from the whole of the Jewel Net is the sum of each of its six billion diamonds. That starry sky, in which you and I shine as brightly as any sun, is our only home.

I n closing, I would like to share with you a guided meditation that I do at the beginning of all my workshops. This meditation is a conscious act of imagination to see your place of work as sacred, and is based on the principle that if you want to bring something good into the world, you first have to imagine it in your mind.

We live in a scientific world that believes in the material basis of things. The phrase "It's all in your mind!" is usually dismissive, mean-

ing "It's not real. It's just your imagination." But take that same phrase—"It's all in your mind!"—and turn it on its head. "It's all in your mind" can also be an affirmation that the imagination is the fountainhead of our entire world. It's all in your mind, everything, in your mind and those of your fellow beings everywhere.

In that spirit, I ask you sit quietly, close your eyes, and empty your mind of all extraneous thoughts. Let your attention settle in your breath, in the rising and falling of your chest and stomach. Rest there for a while, until your mind is clear, like a painter's white canvas before it is touched by the first stroke of the brush.

Now picture your place of work as it appears from the outside. See it as you would

See your workplace as holy, and all the people in it as holy.

when you first approach it every morning. (If you work at home, picture your house from the outside, as you would see it when you come back from a walk.) In all likelihood the actual building is rather nondescript. Perhaps it is an office high-rise or a low-slung factory floor. If you work out-of-doors, perhaps it is a staging area or a dispatching shed.

In any case, allow your imagination to alter your image of this place. Give it a different roof, the roof of a church or temple. See its architecture as reflecting your spiritual ideals.

Now imagine yourself entering the place and going inside. The room where you work is empty. Your colleagues have not yet arrived. Cast the gaze of your imagination around the room. In real life, no doubt your workplace is filled with the usual clutter, papers in piles on desks, stacks of uncollected transmissions in a jumble next to the fax machine, emptied trash cans left out by the janitorial staff. (If you work at home, perhaps your home office, which no one else sees, is even messier!) Against this mundane tableau, superimpose a different image, that of the inside of a temple or church. Imagine the feeling you have when you step inside such a temple and visualize that feeling pervading your place of work.

Now imagine your coworkers entering and taking their places, one by one. If you work at home, imagine the people you deal with as customers, as clients, as phone, fax, or e-mail correspondents, taking their places in whatever part of the country or world they live and work. At first, you see them as they usually are. Some of them are your friends. Some of them annoy you. Others you do not know well, or at all. There is your boss, late as usual, weaving her way through the desks and cubicles to a private office. About each of these people, with whom you spend more time each day than anyone else in your life, you have some opinion, some like or dislike.

As these people take their places, set those customary attitudes and opinions aside. Imagine that a different kind of visual power opens up within you, so that you can see your coworkers not as they appear on the outside but as they really are. Let that nature show itself as a shining jewel in the middle of each person's forehead, glowing with a soft, pleasing light. Imagine the whole room (or shop floor, or construction site, or restaurant kitchen) being lit up by this subtle light. Your coworkers are going about their ordinary tasks, seemingly unaware of this luminosity. But you can see it, because you choose to see it, because you want to see it, as a conscious act of spiritual intention.

Sustain this vision for a few minutes. See your workplace as holy, and all the people in it as holy. The materialist, the skeptic in us, may whisper: "This is not the way things REALLY are. This is just my fantasy, my imagination." The spiritual life within you responds: "This IS the way things really are, and the ordinary way we see has a veil that hides it from us."

Remember, "It's all in your mind!"

Because you choose to sustain this vision of your workplace and your workmates, it is as real as anything is.

Now, slowly, one person at a time, allow the chairs to empty, the room to thin out, until once again you are alone in the empty space. It is the end of the day; you are the last one to leave. You go out the front door (or the door to your home office), mentally shutting the windows and turning out the lights. Before you go, you turn back and look once more at the work space from the outside. The church or temple roof your imagination has given it now fades away. The building is once again as it was.

You allow the vision to dissipate and slowly disappear. Once again the canvas of your mind is blank. You allow your attention to return to the rising and falling of your breath.

How do you feel? Is some small, disillusioned voice whispering, "I don't know about that jerk so-and-so. He sure doesn't have any diamond in HIS forehead!"

That is the complexity and wonder of our human condition. The annoying and the uplifting, the sacred and the profane, the profound and the trivial, the meaningful and the meaningless, all coexist in our lives, like the inhabitants of a small town or village. We don't all necessarily like each other. Sometimes we might even want to kill each other. But we share the same fate. We dream the same dreams. And without each other, we are nothing.

I will end as I began, by quoting one last time my teacher Harry

Roberts, who said, "To find joy in your work is the greatest thing for a human being." If that is true, if work deserves to be more than just a living, then how can we find a way not just to find joy in our work but to make that joy abundant, so that it can be shared by everyone?

> *May all beings be awake.*
> *May all beings be happy.*
> *May all beings be at peace.*

UNIVERSAL PRAYER FOR THE
WELFARE OF ALL BEINGS

Lewis Richard is a Buddhist teacher, workshop leader, software entrepreneur, and musician/composer. Formerly executive vice president of Smith & Hawken, Ltd., he is the founder and owner of Forerunner Systems, Inc., the leading provider of inventory management software to the catalog industry. *Lake of No Shore,* his debut solo piano album, was released by Artifex Records in February 1999. An ordained disciple of Buddhist master Shunryu Suzuki Roshi, Mr. Richmond co-leads Dharma Friends, a meditation group in his hometown of Mill Valley, California.